"Calvin Roberson has written a powerful and practical book that is deceptively easy to read. Just about every sentence has a jewel in it—easily understood and applicable to the daily needs of a committed relationship. Pastor Cal's insights translate immediately into ways we can protect and improve even a troubled marriage—if we practice his version of 'CPR.' I can't imagine anyone, single or married, who would not be inspired, or would not profit, from the wisdom in this book."

—Pepper Schwartz, PhD, *New York Times* bestselling author of *The Normal Bar: The Surprising Secrets of Happy Marriages*

"As a prominent urban radio host, we talk about relationships a lot on our shows and when it's time to call on an expert, there aren't too many 'experts' I trust who talk the talk, walk the walk, and lead by example—but Pastor Cal is it. As we say, he's the GOAT (greatest of all time) when it comes to marriage and relationship insight. *Marriage Ain't for Punks* is consistent to what we love and trust about Pastor Cal. It's realistic, honest (brutally, when needed), and practical. I honestly wish I had the type of guidance shared in this book a few years back...but I'm glad I have it now."

—Nina Brown, radio and TV host

"I'm not a huge fan of counseling, but Pastor Cal makes me look at it differently. He's such a down-to-earth guy and breaks things down in a way that empowers you and makes you want to better yourself. He's revolutionizing the game and is a brother I can get down with on the counseling tip."

—Ty Law, Pro Football Hall of Fame class of 2019

MARRIAGE AIN'T FOR PUNKS

MARRIAGE AIN'T FOR PUNKS

*A No-Nonsense Guide
to Building a Lasting
Relationship*

CALVIN ROBERSON

New York Nashville

FaithWords
Hachette Book Group
1290 Avenue of the Americas, New York, NY 10104
faithwords.com
twitter.com/faithwords

First Edition: September 2021

FaithWords is a division of Hachette Book Group, Inc. The FaithWords name and logo are trademarks of Hachette Book Group, Inc.

The publisher is not responsible for websites (or their content) that are not owned by the publisher.

The Hachette Speakers Bureau provides a wide range of authors for speaking events. To find out more, go to www.hachettespeakersbureau.com or call (866) 376-6591.

Library of Congress Cataloging-in-Publication Data has been applied for.

ISBNs: 978-1-5460-1569-7 (hardcover); 978-1-5460-1570-3 (ebook)

Printed in the United States of America

LSC-C

Printing 1, 2021

To all the couples who thought marriage would have been easier and happier and didn't punk out until it was.

Contents

Introduction

They literally bumped into each other at a conference, and the rest was history. Two go-getters seeking marital momentum.

Rae was a rising star in her career as an IT technician. She was intelligent, powerful, and well respected for her knowledge and leadership. Her five-foot three, super-toned, alluringly beautiful exterior often threw people off guard. Coworkers sometimes made the mistake of assuming she was docile or petite. Nothing could be further from the truth! She had literally beaten all the odds in emerging from her Chattanooga, Tennessee, trailer-park upbringing to become an elegant and educated powerhouse in her field. Her goal was to break every glass ceiling she encountered, and she was well on her way to doing just that.

Jesse had been a nerd his whole life. As a loner in high school, he opted out of sports to focus on his hobby, the financial markets. He wasn't the handsomest or even the most intelligent, but nobody could match his intensity and focus. He was a plain-looking guy at five feet, ten inches tall with a slight frame. But he did have an understated rugged look. And because of his dogged persistence and intense attention to detail, he had done exceptionally well as a tech company analyst. He often noticed attractive women, but never had the confidence or the time to approach them.

That's when Jesse bumped into Rae. He was turning a corner

as she was rushing into the same meeting to get a good seat—boom! He accidentally knocked her phone out of her hand.

"Whoa, I am so sorry!" Jesse exclaimed, bending down and inspecting the phone to make sure it wasn't broken. He handed it back with his best smile.

Rae's frustration quickly subsided because of his respectful and repentant behavior. She even smiled back to calm his fears. It was only a brief moment, but it was enough to pique both their interests in the possibility of having a less awkward chance to be properly introduced. That chance happened after the meeting when Rae intentionally walked past him and playfully jerked her phone away, as if avoiding another crash. He laughed, they talked, and as I said—the rest was history.

Two years later, they were married. Jesse's nerdy looks had been markedly transformed by Rae into a Wall Street hunk. She was steadily moving up in her career. They had settled into married life, complete with a new home and shared friends. Their chance meeting had given them both what neither had been looking for.

You might expect these two powerhouses to make an awesome power team as husband and wife. But as time went on, they began to drift into a common marriage routine. At the end of the day, when they both turned down the volume on their busy lives, they found they didn't have much energy left for each other. After nearly six years of marriage, they frustrated easily and chose to spend time on their computers researching rather than relating to one another.

Occasionally they would get a call from their respective work colleagues to discuss the next day's plans. Whoever took the call would perk up, showing more interest in achieving greatness in their career than in their relationship. The juices would flow, and the energy would ignite. But as soon as the interaction was over, they'd settle back into the tension of their marriage once again.

If you were to look at Rae and Jesse as they sat in their living room—physically together but emotionally light-years apart—what would you see? A failed relationship? Spouses in name only? A marriage on the rocks?

Not me. I see an opportunity for something great.

THE TRUTH ABOUT MARRIAGE

In my almost twenty-five years as a marriage counselor, I've learned that great marriages don't begin until you're ready to walk out the door. When you look at your husband and literally feel sick at what you see. When she leaves for work and you wish she'd never come home. You get nauseous at arguing about the same crap over and over again. You don't want to be touched. You would rather spend the night in the backyard than sleep in the bed with him. You feel as though this was the biggest mistake of your life.

Have you ever felt like that? If you've been married or you're married now, I'll bet the honest answer is yes. As a marriage second-timer, I understand the pain of a failed relationship. In my youth, I did not have the skills or knowledge to know how to navigate the difficulties of marriage. I found out quickly and painfully that matrimony without preparation or sufficient education will end in failure and regret.

These experiences are painful and real. Relationship counselors, marriage gurus, and self-help books will instruct you to speak your spouse's love language or learn the seven principles of a successful marriage. They may tell you that men are from Mars and women are from Venus. These approaches might work for some marriages, but usually they only put a Band-Aid on the gushing wound of a challenged relationship. In truth, sometimes the hemorrhaging is necessary.

Here is the reality: There are no secrets to making marriage work. There are as many love languages as there are human emotions. You may never enjoy the image you concocted of what a happy or beautiful marriage looks like or what great kids look like. Rather, your journey toward a successful marriage may include much of the following:

- You are so dog-tired of each other that your sex life becomes inactive or uninspiring.
- You may, in some cases, be tempted to hurt each other physically.
- You forget about communication boundaries and say whatever is on your mind because you are fed up.
- The kids hear you argue and feel their world is falling apart.
- You enjoy it when another person flirts with you; you may even initiate it!
- There are tears, there may be cursing, and there could even be screaming.
- Prayers may help, but don't take away the pain.

Conventional wisdom says that's a marriage on its last leg. About to crash and burn. Absolutely not! On the contrary, this is a marriage laying the foundation for a beautiful reset. These are relationships that have just entered the flaming crucible of marriage reality and have begun the arduous task of streamlining and fitting two completely different personalities together.

The trick is for couples to effectively crack the surface of their emotions and see past the romanticism and fantasy of their unrealistic expectations. When they do that, they will understand how their union, if managed carefully, can create positive legacies and change lives for generations. They will realize that they have started something beautiful, even though it may not appear so at the time. And they will learn that nothing great comes as a result of mediocrity and calm.

Successful marriages are made of victorious people who understand the goal is not euphoria. The goal is not to emulate the perfect sitcom relationship where everything is wonderful again after each thirty-minute episode. They don't romanticize the relationship. They don't mask their problems. Instead, they run toward them, ferociously attacking each challenge head on with a never-lose attitude. They realize the remarkable power they have together, and no issue, challenge, or terror has the power to dismantle what they are constructing.

THE TRUTH ABOUT THIS BOOK

Over the years, I have emerged as a stand-out voice on relationship success. One reason for that is because I understand marriage is not a time or a space to be politically correct—it's too important. I believe tough love really works in today's relationships. While I've weathered some criticism for instructing couples to push past their fanciful ideas of *feeling* in love and fight to *grow* in love, I believe the success speaks for itself.

Marriage Ain't for Punks brings that same energy and no-nonsense audacity onto the page. It is not a book on "tips for a great marriage." It is not a manifesto on nuptial happiness that, if followed, will turn your relationship into a little slice of heaven on earth. I intentionally shy away from gimmicks, tricks, or pablum commonly used to make marriage work.

In fact, the idea of this book is not to make marriage work.

That's right: Marriage is not the thing that is supposed to work. People are supposed to work! Marriage is simply the vehicle they have chosen to be in, but every marriage must have willing participants who understand that this institution may sometimes feel like an actual institution. It is not the remedy for loneliness. It is not the gold-paved avenue leading to a rainbow, complete with balloons and a pot of gold. Marriage can be tough, and the only thing that stands between you and divorce is your sheer will to fight like hell and manage your own feelings.

> **Marriage is not the thing that is supposed to work. People are supposed to work!**

Truly, of all the things in life people have attempted, failed at, attempted again, and still experienced the most miserable of results, marriage stands at the top of the list. For as many people who fail at it, the question looms: Why in the world would you even want to do it? Why spend countless hours arguing about the same dumb issues again and again just to make up, have great makeup sex, and then a few days later argue again about—you guessed it—the same problem?

I believe there is something that intrinsically exists in this mysterious thing called marriage that draws us like moths to an oncoming headlight. We have positive and fanciful expectations in spite of the numerous examples of train wreck marriages we've either witnessed or experienced.

Now suffice it to say, not all marriages are or will be this dire or desperate. In fact, a great number of marriages may never experience the impact of the moth flying to its doom. Many couples have done serious work on themselves and have learned how to communicate openly and honestly and can successfully navigate the challenges they face.

These positive relationships are what we admire. These are the stories of grandparents who have been married for fifty-plus years and are enjoying their golden years, hand in hand. These are the role models who give us hope and inspire us to pursue this blessed institution with great anticipation.

We still want the fairy tale—the happily ever after—and we rightfully believe we can have it! Even for those who are still licking their nuptial wounds after serious *marital arts* battles and have declared they're completely done with marriage, there is a small seed still planted somewhere in their psyche that, if given the slightest nourishment, will start to grow into the possibility that maybe next time it can work.

Okay, I must admit it: I'm one of those who believe. I believe in the fantasy, the unreal expectations, and the fairy-tale endings. But believing in them does not mean they will happen all at once. In fact, most of the time they come in segments. The key to a healthy marriage is to choose wisely, move thoughtfully, and commit permanently.

Easy? Absolutely not. But then again, marriage ain't for punks!

CHAPTER 1

Profiling a Punk

As a kid, I weighed barely a hundred pounds, dripping wet. Chucky was easily twice my size and five years older with a mean streak as big as his protruding forehead. So knocking me literally on my butt in our pickup basketball game on the dusty home-made court was an easy feat. But then, it was a part of what we did as country kids.

And as quickly as I hit the ground, I bounced back up in his face, trying to block his shot. It was laughable to watch. It was like watching an advancing great white shark going after its prey, unaware that an annoying little suckerfish was attached to its fin, flailing about, trying to stop it.

It was all a part of the game. That is, until Chucky decided to further exert his dominance by using my feeble attempts to block to make a public spectacle out of me. After successfully making his shot, he brashly turned around, pushed me to the ground, and uttered the word that changed the game entirely.

"Get outta here, punk!"

As the incendiary words dripped from his arrogant, curled lips, they seemed to ignite something in me. Instantaneously, my hundred-pound frame grew to three times its size. My strength was that of a hundred men. My anger was unchecked, and it felt as if I could actually fly.

Actually, my anger was real, but the flying I imagined was me being tossed by Chucky over a barbed wire fence. But in my defense, I bounced up and returned to the fight. After all, it was required to prove I wasn't a punk!

While growing up in our small but tough Southern town, there were three things you couldn't tell me or any of my friends without getting a quick and sometimes vicious reaction. You could not disdainfully spout the words "Yo' mama!" You could not *double-dare* anyone. And you could never call any guy a "punk." Not unless you were ready to seriously scrap.

The word "punk" meant you were not a real man, even at twelve years old. It meant you were not up for the challenge; that you were an inferior or unimpressive person who simply did not have the nerve to face whatever imminent danger presented itself. And to accept this emasculating insult without some kind of bravado and male posturing would only further prove you deserved the insult in the first place. This was serious, because who wants to feel they don't measure up? Who wants to face the truth that they can't accomplish a certain thing or that they aren't up to the task?

We all want to believe we have this indomitable force within us like latent nitroglycerin just waiting to be shaken by someone who challenges us to perform. It would be great to have superpowers bestowed upon us by some otherworldly force in the outer reaches of the universe, to be activated when we've reached the absolute end of our rope. Then, at last, it bursts forth in unrelenting splendor and accomplishes the impossible.

The truth is, the great majority of us do have power that lies beneath the surface. Power that has been created within us, yet we have never accessed. It's dormant and waiting to be exercised. We have heard stories or maybe even witnessed some of the astonishing feats of people trapped in horrible situations who choose to suffer personal injury to save themselves or the lives of others. We've seen it in the recorded incidents of mothers who lift heavy objects to rescue their trapped and suffering children. The list goes on with the incredible deeds that people perform under extreme cases of duress.

But that list tends to shorten drastically when it comes to the superhuman strength or willpower needed to salvage or save our personal relationships.

As of the most recent census, the divorce rate has continued to decline, reaching a forty-year low, according to the National Center for Family and Marriage at Bowling Green University. This means couples are staying in marriages longer. More and more people are attempting to find resolution and actually want to stay married.

However, another reason for the declining divorce rate is that the number of young people who have never married is at an all-time high, according to a recent survey by the Pew Research Center. Nearly one in five adults ages twenty-five and older has never been married. This may indicate that many are losing faith in the possibility of a successful marriage.

To me, this is a clear indicator that most don't choose to access their inner power and work at marriage, but rather simply resolve to *punk out* on what is arguably the most important venture any person can undertake in a lifetime. Often, the same type of verve and vigor we invest in reaching life goals is unavailable or even unconsidered when it comes to our relationships. We seem to think if we just believe in love, then all things will work out. If we simply care enough, our relationship will somehow find its sweet spot and will evolve into this beautiful and satisfying fairy tale.

This can't be further from the truth. Of all the endeavors two people can embark upon, the idea of blending two distinct personalities so they can move together in the same successful direction has to be the most difficult ever imagined—and the one that needs the most attention.

In over two decades of counseling people on various levels of relationship conflict, I have found there is a ripple effect that begins with one's ability to manage and resolve difficulties in their relationships, and then spreads to other areas of their lives. I believe a person's ability to find happiness and effectiveness in their job, in their school, and even in their health can all be linked to whether their relationships contribute to or detract from their lives. And when you consider that marriage is the most intense and closest relationship possible, the effect on other areas of life can be enormous.

More often than not, people stroll into adult marriage situations while maintaining the mentality and lack of commitment of adolescents. They don't count (or don't know how to count) all the costs associated with plunging into that colossal decision. In our modern, quick-fix society, it is easier to give up than to persevere—easier to throw in the towel than to push beyond our boundaries. Nowhere is this seen more obviously than in marriage. Mole hills that could be resolved with guidance or counseling are often inflated into what couples feel are impenetrable mountains.

Most marriages I have encountered have not taken advantage of premarital counseling. For some strange reason, people feel as though they will just know what to do when they get married. There they are, standing hand in hand and listening to the officiant or reciting their own vows and believing this will be a heaven on earth. This is the hope. But after the wedding night sex (and trust me, there is *no* greater anticipated sex than wedding night sex), it's not long before the dust settles and the first real issues raise their ugly heads.

Even with couples who have lived together for years prior to a wedding, there is still a change that happens when they get married. Somehow, hearing those words "I now pronounce you husband and wife" sets off a mystical chemical reaction in the brain, and a new reality begins. The person you thought you knew actually left you at the altar. It's all different now. This is when the earliest signs of marriage punkery begin to appear.

Punks are neither male nor female; they have no race or ethnicity. Punkery bypasses all those social classifications. This is where I have seen many couples plant the first seeds of doubt in their relationships, and where those seeds take root and begin to grow. They soon begin to view each other as enemies instead of partners.

In my decades of rescuing couples from the brink of divorce, I've found that a great number of hopefuls are quick to choose the path of least resistance. They will walk away from fixable difficult situations, as opposed to rolling up their nuptial sleeves and battling the challenges. I've heard reasons that are as varied as the personalities involved, but whatever they are, they still amount to punking out.

One excuse I often hear is this: *He'll never change, because people don't change.* The idea that people can't evolve into something better is completely contradictory to who we are as humans. Throughout the vast millennia of life on earth, people have always learned from their mistakes and failures and course-corrected. The ability to change is deeply tied to who we are as intelligent beings on this planet.

Another reason I've heard people use to punk out is that a certain offense is unforgivable. While there may be things done that cause severe damage, I've counseled numerous couples who have made the decision to stay together and mutually fight through rather than give up. This has only made their relationships stronger.

Now, don't get me wrong. I'm not so naïve as to believe that every problem can be fixed. However, the common issues that most couples deal with on a daily basis can be resolved. Issues like anger, ineffective communication, or the common excuse that you *love her, but you're just not in love with her* are all the result of not having the necessary tools and the right perspective to confront, analyze, and solve these fixable challenges.

THE TWO SIDES OF MARRIAGE

Marriage is supposed to make you better. When done right, marriage is supposed to be that thing that propels you and your spouse into your mutual destiny. It is not an antiquated social construct as some have claimed. Rather, successful marriages are at the root of a stable society. They are necessary to show that commitment is more than words; marriage is legally obligating yourself, your time, and your resources to another person—with the same thing being given back to you.

Marriage can be the most difficult and the easiest thing in the world, sometimes at the same time. There are two sides to marriage. Let's look at them individually.

The first side of marriage is the ugly or difficult side. With all the books and seminars available on sharing the "secrets" to a successful marriage, one would think this marriage thing would be a breeze. However, divorce rates and miserable marriages tell a different story. They tell the story of well-meaning people who are attempting a noble and time-honored thing, yet ultimately find themselves sleeping at opposite sides of the bed, deliberately trying not to touch each other. Sometimes they resort to living as roommates instead of love mates, having sexual fantasies about other relationships, or finding solace in scrolling through their smart devices peering at nameless faces or naked bodies.

When you find yourself in this phase of marriage, understand that it is just that: a phase. Often, I will see husbands and wives encounter difficult times in their relationship and will immediately magnify those trials as though they are the totality of the relationship. They will make decisions about the entire marriage based on segments of time where they are having problems.

No one does this in any other areas of their lives. My wife and I have a few favorite restaurants we frequent. Sometimes, we have a less than great experience at one of them. We simply chalk it up to maybe the chef is having an off day. But because we know the totality of his expertise, we would never write the restaurant off our list. That's *throwing the baby out with the bath water.*

The same can be said of going through the negative phase of marriage. It is vital that every couple understands the inevitable reality that there will be bad days, weeks, or months. There may be arguments that rival world wars. You will sleep on opposite sides of the bed. You may wonder why you married in the first place. And you will make stupid mistakes that seemingly take forever to recover from. But these are not the marriage. They are only one side of it—a phase that is intended to teach you both the value of hunkering down, fighting the problem together, digging deeper, and discovering the beauty in the ashes.

But there is also the second side of marriage. It is the positive, much more exciting phase of the relationship. It is the story of couples who have been married for decades and still find themselves involuntarily drawn to touch each other, just to feel close. This side of marriage tells the story of those who can't wait to get home from business trips. They feel as though making love with their spouse gets better each time. They don't need other friends or companions around to have fun. They are satisfied with just the two of them. They have financial challenges, unruly children, and job pressures, but they join together to attack the problem instead of letting the problem attack their marriage.

I have been privileged to see so many couples experience the beauty and joy of nuptial bliss. In most of those cases, the couples have made the decision to be okay with not being perfect. They understand that the person they are married to is a blessing to them. They realize the value of having someone in their life who knows their deepest secrets and will take those cherished secrets with them to the grave.

They have their own unspoken language and can sense private humor without saying a word and then spontaneously laugh in sync. They understand that there are valuable stories behind each other's blemishes and imperfections. Stories that they each honor and respect, which increase their value to one another.

This is the side or phase of marriage that hopeful singles dream of when they think of spending their lives with their beloved. This is the fairy-tale phase. This is what love stories and romantic comedies emphasize, and it's what we all aspire to have.

How is the latter phase different from the former? The latter has discovered the hard-learned fact that anything worth having is worth sacrificing to achieve! They have learned that with transparency and effective communication, every challenge can be met head on, fully examined, and solved. Every success can be completely celebrated, and true love can be completely realized.

Furthermore, every couple who has experienced the blissfully beautiful side of marriage understands that it has evolved out of the ugly and difficult phases. The splendor of these relationships stands like a lotus flower, which can achieve its astounding beauty only from the mud and mire it uses as its foundation. It must have the difficult and the undesirable times in order to produce the positive and successful results.

Relationships must go through conflict without fearing that it will destroy them. Dissention doesn't mean it's the end of the marriage, or that something is seriously wrong because you argue. On the contrary, conflict has a goal. It is a vehicle that, when used properly, can lead to understanding and mutual respect.

In order to move from the negative phases of marriage to the more beautiful and satisfying plateaus, there are steps to getting there. There are intentional decisions and

> Anyone can have a wedding and be legally bound, but it doesn't truly become a marriage until you've cried, argued, regretted, despised, then rethought, forgiven, changed, loved deeper, and committed over and over again.

actions that must be carried out. Here is the unapologetic truth: Anyone can have a wedding and be legally bound, but it doesn't truly become a marriage until you've cried, argued, regretted, despised, then rethought, forgiven, changed, loved deeper, and committed over and over again.

CHAPTER 2

Marital CPR

Reuben and Selena were counting the days to when the last of their four children would finally move out of the house and they could enjoy empty nesting. Oddly, a number of couples dread the prospect of being all alone after the kids leave, but not these two. In fact, among their friends, they were truly a mystery. How does anyone married for thirty-four years still act as though they're newlyweds?

Often Reuben and Selena would snuggle up together, his hand unconsciously massaging her neck, or her fingers rubbing his earlobe. After all those years they genuinely enjoyed each other's presence, and they had no problem talking about their love life. You would think they were taking some sort of hormone supplements to keep them energized, but anyone who witnessed their love could see it was authentic. This was how their marriage had evolved.

It wasn't always this way. In fact, there was a time when they thought it was over. They'd been married only six years when they reached an emotional impasse. Their second child had just been born and they were experiencing serious financial troubles. Reuben lost his job and decided he wouldn't work for anyone anymore. Selena didn't understand and felt completely unsupported. Mainly because her dad, whom she looked up to, had retired after thirty years in the automotive industry. It was a man's duty to get a job and stay in it, she felt.

Reuben was convinced otherwise and knew he had to branch out on his own. Selena felt she was not being heard and started having intimate conversations with an old boyfriend. Although it never led to physical intimacy, it was enough to cause serious trouble in their marriage. Reuben actually confronted her paramour, which led to the end of that potential affair.

After counseling, Reuben and Selena were able to reboot their marriage and gain a new perspective on their needs and desires. Though it took a while, the relationship they grew after their challenges was more satisfying than they ever could have imagined.

They learned a lesson I refer to as *Marital CPR*, which stands for "commitment, passion, and respect." That is how they were able to breathe life into what could have been a lifeless existence together. They were able to find the key to their success by realizing the value of what they had built and by intentionally doing the work necessary to make their marriage work.

Marital CPR is the building block of any healthy marriage. All three elements must exist not only for a marriage to grow, but for it to thrive.

COMMITMENT

The first principle is *commitment*. It's a term we use often in our careers, in sports, or in other areas of our lives where steadfastness is required. But commitment is also vital for any successful marriage.

Here's how I define commitment: *It is the state of being bound emotionally or intellectually to a course of action or to another person.* In essence, commitment is a purely intellectual and/or emotional decision to stay in a situation "come hell or high water." A commitment is a contract entered into by two mutually agreeing parties to uphold standards and abide by principles, and to make certain that each person receives the agreed-upon satisfaction in that document or agreement.

I have often heard people laud their commitment to different things in their lives, but one of my most memorable examples of unwavering commitment was from my youth. A number of my friends and I played football in a city league. I remember the adrenaline-charged feeling of suiting up and running out on the field as the handful of spectators, parents mostly, cheered us on. Now, to be honest, we were only mediocre at best. As I recall, our coach didn't expect college scouts to be at any of our games. We never won any championships and didn't make any playoffs. In fact, we were not even the most committed people on the field. That proud distinction went to the cheerleaders, most of whom were the sisters and friends of the team.

I distinctly remember one game in particular where we were losing by a mile. That happened often, but it never deterred our cheerleaders. One repetitive cheer in their limited repertoire gave the perfect summation for commitment. Irrespective of the score, they would rhythmically clap to the chant "That's all right, that's okay, we're gonna beat 'em anyway."

To be honest, it became annoying after a while. Everyone in the stadium was well aware we were losing. We didn't have a chance. But the cheerleaders droned on like the musicians playing on the sinking *Titanic*, "That's all right, that's okay, we're gonna beat 'em anyway."

This kind of dogged persistence in the face of failure is what commitment looks like. It doesn't consider the dire circumstances, but holds out hope until the very end.

Reuben and Selena were able to make their marriage work because they simply did not accept failure as an option. They felt they could tackle any issue and dismantle it for the sake of staying together.

This is not a common mindset for modern marriages. Commitment is sometimes seen as conditional. As in, "I'm committed as long as..." or, "I'm committed if..." While these caveats are understandable, they do not illustrate what true commitment really is. It falls short of the mark.

Of course, there are exceptions to every rule. No one should have unswerving devotion to an abuser or to someone who will put your life, family, or emotional health in jeopardy. But when these dire circumstances don't exist, a couple should make the intentional decision to dedicate themselves to finding every opportunity to succeed.

When a couple says they are committed to the marriage, that declaration requires them to accept the principle that ending a marriage is seldom the solution to a problem. To end a marriage instead of resolving the problems will simply create baggage, which will only be transferred to some other future relationship.

I have sat in front of many couples who declare they can't make it beyond their issues. *This is too much*, they exclaim. However, most of us would never consider leaving our children as a solution to the problems they present. We choose to stay in our kids' lives and see them through their issues. The same tenacity should exist between the people who brought the children into the world.

True commitment says you don't even introduce the option of divorce. I counsel couples never to bring up the option of separation or divorce. Barring abuse or cruelty, it is a coward's way out. It should never be an option on the table, and this is what my wife and I live by.

I've held a few high corporate positions. I've experienced the feeling that accompanies the realization that it's time to move on to another job. When most people seriously consider leaving their job to take another one, their devotion and performance in their current job will suffer. It's a natural response. Why would you give all your dedication when you're thinking about leaving?

The same is true in marriage. When you plant the seed of possibly leaving, it will grow with or without any further nurturing. The possibility of not having to confront the struggles and conflicts of the current relationship acts like an anesthetic to numb you from giving your full effort. That's why it is important never to consider leaving your marriage. Simply don't say it! This is at the root of the promise to commit: the idea that you won't allow the option of leaving to even enter your mind.

When it comes to commitment in a relationship, you must decide at the onset that you are in it for life. If your destination is not determined, you are prone to make changes in a direction that appears to lead to more interesting or pleasant places. Your destination in marriage is *'til death do you part.* That is the agreement. Anything short of that, barring the exceptions mentioned above, is not real commitment.

I know this is tough for a lot of people. I've had many frustrated spouses ask me, "How do I stay committed?"

> Commitment is a constant decision, not a onetime choice. Each day, you build on the decision you made the day before.

The answer is by deciding to do so every day. Commitment is a constant decision, not a onetime choice. Each day, you build on the decision you made the day before. You must actually verbalize your decision to your spouse and to yourself. It's a constant reassurance when your mate hears that you are in the relationship for the long haul. And each time you state your decision to stay, you are building your own resolve as well. After a while, these constant reminders will become a part of the fabric of your relationship. Eventually, commitment becomes a habitual and unconscious way of life.

At this point, it won't matter if you *feel* committed.

Too often, we depend on how we feel to indicate if we're committed to a certain thing. Feelings, however, are vacuous and fleeting. They can't be counted on and are subject to changing based on possibly what you had for breakfast that morning or whether you got enough sleep the night before.

In our current society, we place a great deal of weight on how we feel about issues. *Trust your feelings. Listen to your heart. The heart wants what it wants.* These are all philosophies we have woven into our understanding of relationships. We have convinced ourselves in many instances to depend on something as unpredictable as a mood.

The heart is synonymous with affections, which again is all about preferences and feelings. We judge our partners based on whether their heart is in the relationship, or whether they feel they are in love. I have seen full-blown arguments develop because someone does or doesn't feel positive about something.

This is unquestionably an ineffective way to tell whether your mate has staying power. In short, you don't have to feel committed to be committed. You decide to dedicate yourself, and you do it regardless of your momentary emotions.

> **In short, you don't have to feel committed to be committed. You decide to dedicate yourself, and you do it regardless of your momentary emotions.**

Now, I'm not going to completely discount emotions. In fact, it is necessary in a relationship to consider the heart in regard to passion and excitement. They are vital in creating the desire to touch and be intimate. Nevertheless, feelings are not what relationship foundations are made of.

Instead, marriage must be founded on something that is unshakable. Something that wades through the murky and turbulent tides of emotions and stands strong, never wavering. The foundation must be dependable. Commitment is that foundation.

Let's talk about the nuts and bolts of commitment. There are two ways to indicate to your partner that you're in the relationship for the duration.

Proactive Displays

A proactive display of commitment is a preemptive manifestation of your desire and intention to be in the relationship for the duration. Think of it as an oath or promise put into action. It is more than just words, but actual things you do to nurture your relationship and create permanency.

These are acts to show your mate that you are *not* leaving. They relay the message that you are establishing long-lasting fixtures in your relationship. While these are not foolproof, they do go a long way to letting your mate know you are serious and that you are digging in and growing roots in the relationship.

Reuben and Selena learned this after their marriage nearly ended. In order for them to assure each other that they were serious, they bought a home together. Nothing shows more seriousness about a relationship than entering a thirty-year mortgage together. Other acts of commitment may include having joint bank accounts, having your spouse as your beneficiary on life insurance or other investment plans, creating holiday traditions together or planning for vacations each year, or even on the lighter side, having scheduled date nights weekly or monthly.

Then there are the verbal statements of commitment. This is when you intentionally communicate to your partner that you'll never leave. Yeah, I said *never*! Or that you're in the relationship 'til death do us part. Simply put, just letting your partner know that your actions and your vows are real. These are all proactive displays.

Passive Displays

Then there are passive displays of commitment. These are the things you avoid doing that may cause insecurity in your relationship. These are acts of omission that assure your spouse of your pledge to be in the relationship. These passive acts are necessary because they allow your spouse to see that you are disciplining yourself. You are shunning bad behavior and those things that may tear at the framework of your marriage.

Some of these may be avoiding questionable friends of the opposite sex. Making sure your spouse is acquainted with your relationships outside the marriage is essential. Whether these are work, church, or social friends, it's important that your spouse is made aware of who you spend time with. You report to your spouse not out of obligation, but rather out of respect.

Another passive display is never to mention divorce, separation, or use other divisive language. Even if you're just being playful with each other, it's unwise to hint at leaving. I've heard many frustrated spouses say to each other things like, "There are other fish in the sea." Or, "I can have anyone I want, but I choose to be with you."

Whether or not these statements are true, they are better left unsaid. These are actually thinly veiled threats that plant seeds in your spouse's mind. And when a disagreement does occur, these seeds will sprout. So do not give your spouse a reason to doubt or question the stability of your marriage. We all know that there may be someone else out there who might want to take on your baggage, but honestly, who cares?

Even the best relationships are vulnerable at some points. We all want to have stability in our lives and have relationships we can depend on. Building the foundation of our relationship by proactively and passively expressing commitment will provide that security we all need.

PASSION

The second principle is *passion*. In its practical sense, passion is a drive or an urge. It's the emotional fuel that motivates us to react with fervor either positively or negatively. It is a mandatory element of loving and successful marriages.

Passion is what keeps your partner coming back for more. It

is what puts that gleam in his eye when she walks through the door, or what makes her do a double take when he dresses in a suit. This hand-holding, eye gazing, butt slapping, sometimes raw emotion is what puts the icing on the cake of the marriage. It may culminate in sex, but even if it does not, the joy of passion is just as satisfying.

This drive and energy help to make marriage fun and interesting. But it also brings with it a great deal of vulnerability and openness. When you are passionate, you are revealing your desires and becoming emotionally naked. I've seen spouses refrain from passion because they don't want to expose their heart. Expressions of uninhibited desire can open a person and make them afraid of whether or not they will be accepted in such a defenseless position.

However, in order to have an exciting marriage, you simply have to push through fears and initiate passion. You can't wait until you feel passion. Sometimes you have to do loving acts irrespective of how you feel and the passionate emotions will often follow.

Married couples often make the mistake of waiting until they feel amorous or loving to do loving acts. The key is to do the actions and the emotions will follow. The opposite doesn't work— when you wait for the feelings before you act. Love is not an emotion; it's a commitment. Once you've committed to love, just know that it's there. You must realize that ultimately passion is under your control. You can initiate it by doing the things that inspire it.

Let's take a look at the actions that precipitate positive passion.

First of all, positive passion lures your mate to you. When you perform positive actions, it softens you both and creates closeness. Such actions let your partner know that you are still in the marriage and send the unquestionable message that says, *I still feel excited about you.* Or, *I think about you when we're away from each other.*

Acts like a passionate caress or holding hands can change an entire mood in a relationship. This shows that you still want to be close. My wife and I make it a habit to hold hands while we're walking. It's something I've had to push myself to do, since I wasn't a big fan of public displays of affection early on. But every habit can be changed. And just because you are not accustomed to touching in public doesn't mean you can't train yourself to do it. Marriage is about both parties changing for the benefit of the whole.

Intentionally saying kind and even sensual words is another way to express positive passion. Simply compliment your mate. Say something good about him or her. Tell them how much you appreciate the progress they're making in their lives and in the marriage. We can never fully appreciate the power of positive affirmation. To simply notice and acknowledge something endearing about your spouse can be seriously mood changing.

Also, selfless acts of kindness require a great deal of vulnerability. I decided when we got married that I would always open the door for my wife. Now trust me, she does *not* need me to open anything for her. She is a very capable and independent woman. However, because of the intent and the emotion behind the gesture, she will stand at the door and wait for me to open it. This shows that she recognizes what I do, and my job is to oblige. It's a small thing that has big dividends.

There can be many acts of kindness from both parties. The object here is to create a habit of kindness. Do things that show you still care; that tell each other that you are still in the relationship for keeps.

On the contrary, negative passion repels. These are the things that are either done or omitted out of apathy or anger. They act as clear indicators that there is a problem in the relationship.

For instance, when you want to punish your spouse by using *the silent treatment*. Shutting down and refusing to speak to your mate is a definite passion killer. Sometimes silence is a stronger communicator than words. When you don't speak, it gives your partner the opportunity for their mind to run wild and imagine what you are feeling. A lot of the time, those ideations are incorrect.

Passion and communication are intrinsically linked. Once cannot exist without the other. In marriage, when communication ends, so does passion. But when it thrives, passion finds its greatest opportunity to express itself. Intimacy is at its height when personal interaction is strong. When a couple has sexual issues, the first thing I ask is, *How is your communication?*

Another act that can exterminate passion is a bad temper or disposition. When a person is volatile and unpredictable, it is nearly impossible to want to be close to them. It simply does not create an environment for intimacy. And the ironic thing is that when a person is reacting this way, the very thing they need is for someone to be close and to help them feel safe enough to be vulnerable.

Anger is a smoke screen that hides an underlying insecurity or sensitivity. It keeps people at bay. In the same stead, it dissipates passion so that there is no fertile ground in which it can grow.

Another passion blocker is a selfish or addictive devotion to other things. I'm referring to people who are unusually dedicated to their careers and have little time for their spouse. Or people who are constantly on social media when those times could be shared learning about each other. Any of these distractions sends the message that something else takes precedence over your mate. This is not to say that dedication to these things is wrong, but when they become all-consuming to the point that they are your first consideration, that's an issue.

I am a huge football fan. I am an unabashed Tennessee Titans fan, and I'm passionate about it. We were living in Nashville when the team first came to the city, and my oldest son and I have been diehard fans ever since. I actually had a room painted in their colors. However, I will easily miss a game or turn off the TV if my wife needs me. She understands that I enjoy following the team and will even support me in my devotion. But she supports me because she knows that family is my top priority. My passion will never be divided, and that decision is completely under my control.

Passion in a marriage can be created or destroyed. It is completely up to the individual as to whether desire exists. When the actions are done and the words are spoken to create passion, then it

> **Passion in a marriage can be created or destroyed. It is completely up to the individual as to whether desire exists.**

will exist. When negative acts are done, passion will die. It's that simple.

RESPECT

The third rung on the Marital CPR ladder is *respect*. This is synonymous with esteem for something or a sense of the worth or excellence about a certain thing. When you respect a certain thing, you venerate it and uphold it as special.

When spouses respect each other, it is evident in the way

they treat each other. You can see it in what they do and in what they refrain from doing. There is an esteem they hold for each other. They have an ease and are unafraid to show emotion and acceptance.

Respect is the ability to value each other and honor the intrinsic worth each brings to the table. You show a high regard for your spouse's intellect and ability to make decisions. You praise the areas where they are compatible to you, and you honor and learn from the areas where they are different from you.

Respect for people is a basic element for living in a normal and well-ordered society.

It is often viewed through the lenses of our upbringing. There may be differences in understanding what respect actually means to your partner because it is subjective. What one person feels might be respectful may not be what the other feels.

A man might feel disrespected if his wife disagrees or debates with him, while the wife was brought up believing that debate and disagreement are healthy. This needs to be discussed thoroughly, and both parties need to discover and reveal what respect looks like to them. A large part of respecting your mate is taking responsibility for what you do wrong and not letting them take the blame.

It is not enough to just *say* you respect a person. When it's truly there, respect cannot be hidden even if it is not expressed. You must show it because of the overwhelming gratitude you have for this person being in your life. It's an involuntary expression, and as such, it produces a reciprocal expression of admiration.

I have seen so much disrespect in couples I've coached that it's heartbreaking. I've found that in a number of instances, people don't realize they are being disrespectful because they have had no real role models of what respect looks like in a relationship. If you respect something, you value it. This means you actually place a price on it. There is an assessment you give it that determines what you are willing to do or give in order to acquire it or keep it.

If a person purchases a beautiful home, the first thing they do is insure it. You want to make sure it's indemnified against loss. Next, you make sure it's presentable and taken care of. You might fix what is broken. You make sure that when visitors come over, they honor your home. They can't act like they own the place. They must respect what is yours. You may even want to show it off to your friends, because you value it. I'm sure you get the point by now.

The same is true in a relationship. When you value your spouse, you take care of them and make sure they are protected. You make sure others don't treat them disrespectfully and you are happy to show them off to your friends. However, the difference here is that you don't own them. They are not your possession, but still your treasure.

Here are some practical questions I have asked couples in regard to showing each other respect in marriage:

- Do you speak positively about each other in public?
- Do you refer to the other in public or private as "raising another child"?
- Is there a mutual admiration of each other's intelligence?
- Are you protective when someone else offends or threatens the other?

These are basic things to consider in regard to respect. But respect cannot be demanded. It must be earned. You don't automatically get it because of your gender or your marital status.

While I believe everyone should respect the institution of marriage, you don't automatically get respect just because you entered the legal agreement.

When a person feels valued or respected, it builds their esteem and opens them up to love freely. It makes them feel worthy of love and motivated to actively participate in the relationship. It is the fertile soil that creates the environment for love to grow. When love is present, respect is a natural outgrowth of it.

In other words, you may respect someone that you don't love, but it's almost impossible to love someone that you don't respect.

Respect can exist on its own without love, but not the other way around. You may respect a public figure, educator, etc. You value their contribution and speak highly of them. Nevertheless, that admiration falls way short of being in love with them. In other words, you may respect someone that you don't love, but it's almost impossible to love someone that you don't respect.

This is because love requires an action. You must respond to love. There is an innate and involuntary thing that happens when you have grown in love with a person. You must do something about how you feel and what you've committed to. A great part of that love response is honoring that person. It is valuing who they are and what they contribute to your life. This is what respect looks like.

To make it more practical, here are some of the direct actions that grow out of love.

Because I value and respect you, I will:

- Care about what you care about.
- Show you by my actions that I'm listening to you.

- Put serious thought into special occasions (birthdays, anniversaries, etc.).

Because I value and respect you, I will not:

- Talk to you like you are a child.
- Do the thing that I KNOW you don't like.
- Insult your intelligence.

I'm sure you can add quite a few more items to the list. But these are examples of how married people act when they are actually in love and find worth in each other. Their actions correspond without having to be requested or prodded. It's natural.

Some may not have been taught how to respect others or simply might not have the tools to show they value their spouse. For example, if a man was never taught to regard another person's opinion, there will be disrespect for any opinion except his own. Or if a woman grew up in a household where respect was not modeled by parents or siblings, she may not be respectful to anyone in her adult life.

This is a fixable problem. The more you allow love to grow and communicate your needs and wants, the more you can learn how to respect another person. We all have the ability to change and learn what we've never been taught. But it takes willingness and vulnerability to do so.

BRINGING IT HOME

Commitment, passion, and respect. They must coexist in a relationship in order for the marriage to thrive. CPR for marriages is like a triangle with each side representing one of these qualities. If one of them is missing, there is a greater chance for the entire structure to collapse.

Without Commitment...

A couple might have a healthy desire for one another because they possess passion. They may want to be around each other and may have a very active sex life. A couple can simply enjoy each other and genuinely like being around each other. Passion can exist on its own. You find this when people are dating. They may mistake passion for love because it feels so good and can go a long way to mimicking real love.

They might also esteem one another. Meaning, they honor who their partner is. They may respect their accomplishments and praise them publicly and privately. Respect can exist without any love upholding it.

But if there is no commitment, they may, inadvertently or deliberately, not care about staying in the marriage. The passion makes it fun and the respect makes them proud, but they don't feel the need to stay and fight for the relationship. They simply don't have staying power and may secretly cheat or just leave altogether.

These are the couples who give themselves loopholes just in case something goes wrong. In a great deal of cases, they will remain faithful—until a better opportunity comes along. This attitude comes from emotional immaturity. That person may not be committed in marriage, or in other areas of his or her life. This may be the mate who has had multiple jobs and always has an excuse for quitting, or other personal relationships ended abruptly without reason.

Without Passion...

A couple may stay together and/or esteem one another, but the attraction will wane, and their marriage will become boring. Unfortunately, a lot of marriages fall into this category. Couples stay together and may actually value and respect one another, but the thrill is gone.

They have *lost that lovin' feeling.* There is no excitement. They do not revel in each other's love. In these cases, a spouse is more likely to cheat or have an emotional affair in order to fulfill that missing element or become complacent and just go through the motions of being married. In each case, the marital union suffers.

Without Respect...

A spouse will remain in the marriage because they are committed. They may even have a satisfying sex life because there is a modicum of passion that exists. But they will not value each other. They will not share in each other's goals and aspirations or esteem one another. As a result, the marriage will become an emotional prison where both parties feel trapped.

A lack of respect may also result in forms of domestic abuse. This may be verbal or physical or both. When someone is not respected, they are treated carelessly and without sincere regard. That spouse is looked upon as an object more than a loving equal and is treated as such.

When all three elements *are* present—commitment, passion, and respect—a relationship can thrive and provide the necessary foundation for success. Those elements become a stable foundation on which to build a lifelong legacy of love and comfort. When any of them are absent, the possibility of a holistic, satisfying relationship is nearly impossible.

For any relationship to thrive in a way that both parties feel appreciated and valued, there must be real, conscious effort. While it's easy to spew words of admiration, the tough, gritty job of making an intellectual decision to stay and work out any difficulty, come hell or high water, is what the marriage requires to progress. It takes the ability to deliberately convince yourself to see beyond imperfections and generate passion, even when you don't feel like it. And it also requires that your significant other recognizes the fact that they are valued; not only with words, but with deeds that indicate such. Sounds tough? Well, it is. Hence, the reason that marriage ain't for punks.

CHAPTER 3

Communicating Like a Punk

Silence has become way too familiar, and tension is an unwelcome, but frequent visitor in their home. Kim usually arrives home first after a full and hectic day of teaching third graders. Her husband, Donnie, shows up later after fighting traffic. She makes sure their teenage twins, a boy and a girl, get their homework done. A couple times a week, she orders out for dinner. The kids actually prefer fast food rather than Mom's cooking, which has become predictable.

There isn't a great deal of communication between Kim and the kids—normally just short questions and answers followed by fake, tolerating smiles from the twins. Kim is happy the kids are communicating at all, but she longs for more. Her only real interaction seems to be with children, and she craves adult contact.

Kim doesn't believe Donnie even likes her anymore. She thinks he loves her, but sometimes he sounds as though he really resents her. Something has been lost. Deadened. He seldom says anything when he comes home. The tension is so thick, she can feel it. She wonders if he's found someone else—or if he even wants to come home.

In Kim's perfect marriage world, Donnie would come home, and they would greet each other with a kiss, take some time to unwind, and then lean on and pour into each other. They'd lie in each other's arms and talk about the day's events. There would be laughter, the twins would come out to join in the fun, and they would all bask in the beauty and joy that is supposed to be *family*. That's her perfect marriage world.

In Donnie's reality, he fights through traffic but still drives around the block a couple times to muster up the mental and emotional strength to come home. He's worked tirelessly managing a call center all day, dealing with irate and unsatisfied customers and employees. He severely dislikes where he is in his career but understands there is a possibility for advancement, so he can't quit. Mortgage, car payments, financial assistance for their aging parents—all these responsibilities tell him he has to keep facing the same reality day after day.

Donnie can't drive all night. At some point, he has to open his front door, cut through the silence, and feel the weight of the anxiety in his home that never seems to go away. When he looks at Kim, he feels as though she is so caught up with school and the kids that he has been put on the back burner. She used to be so into him, but something has changed. Now when they go to bed, it's only to sleep. They both feel it's better to just get on their phones or watch TV rather than face the uncomfortable awkwardness of trying to touch each other. Their communication consists of only a few emotionless words—the words of strangers. So they take to their opposite sides of the bed and try to drift off to sleep, only to awaken to the same reality the next day.

In Donnie's perfect marriage world, he'd come home and hear laughter as he approached the door. He would enter, and the twins' faces would light up as they ran to give him hugs. He would embrace them, but his true joy would come from the passionate embrace of his wife. He would feel peace within the walls. Home would be his refuge. He and Kim would embrace each other at night, and when sex did happen, it would be incredible.

COMMUNICATION IS KEY

A great number of the couples who have plodded into my office with dejected looks on their faces all have one common denominator in their complaints: They don't feel like they communicate. Of course, after speaking with them for a while, I have found that nothing could be further from the truth. The fact is, all of them communicate their feelings often and deeply. They just don't realize it.

Look at the example of Kim and Donnie. They are relaying feelings and opinions in volumes. The way they look at each other conveys deep meanings. What they don't say can say quite a bit. Their motions and gestures, their expressions and posture are all speaking loudly. The question is whether what they are communicating is building up or destroying.

I believe people communicate the way they have been communicated to. Surprisingly, that's usually true even if they don't like the way they've been communicated to their entire lives. Maybe you were bullied as a student or a child. Maybe, like me, you were often told to shut up or stop talking so much. Or maybe you were ignored for a great deal of your upbringing. Whatever the communication was that you received early in life, that became the standard for you.

Some of the biggest marital challenges in couples I have counseled have been in this area. Many quiet and resentful nights followed by tense mornings have come out of ineffective communication, even though couples know better. And once resolution is postponed because of pride or arrogance, the tension builds, the walls go up, and it takes serious personal effort to man up or woman up and break the ice and simply say something that isn't mean-spirited or provoking.

This is not an easy task. It takes an enormous amount of marbles to muster up the energy and suppress the pride to humbly open the lines of communication, but then again, marriage ain't for punks!

If you want a beautiful marriage, the first thing to do is determine the right way to speak to your partner.

THE SEVEN PATHWAYS OF COMMUNICATION

Have you ever met someone who seems to know just the right words to say, and even more, just the right way to convey them so that seemingly everyone wants to hear the coveted jewels that flow from their mouth? Over the years, I have studied how people communicate and why some people are just simply more effective than others. Some are able to say exactly what needs to be said at the exact time it needs to be said.

I teach couples that there are seven pathways to effective communication. These are the means by which we relay our thoughts and emotions to the people around us. This is how we let people know how we truly feel.

We may have countless opinions and feelings that constantly run through our mind every minute. These thoughts, as random as they are, must have some form of outward expression. They must have an outlet. Sometimes the expression may be voluntary, or it may be unintentional. But believe me, your inward feelings will eventually reach the surface and your spouse will know how you truly feel!

The pathways of communication are the avenues through which your emotions are being relayed. Once we understand how we're communicating, then we can control what we're communicating. Those pathways are our words, tone, gestures, eyes, written communication, touch, and silence.

> **Once we understand how we're communicating, then we can control what we're communicating.**

Words

The first pathway of communication is the words we say.

When I was in high school, my favorite English teacher, Ms. Spence, introduced me to the power and proficiency of words. We were studying Shakespeare, and I was lost between the *theretos* and the *whitherfores*. She patiently encouraged me to read slowly and look at the context of the story. She showed me that words were a tool. They were valuable and instrumental in transforming my unheard thoughts and feelings into an audible reality.

But the first thing I needed was to learn words. So I started to study synonyms. I read the dictionary and worked to make sure I always had more than one word to convey a particular thought. Even at an early age, I wanted my thoughts, as juvenile as they were at the time, to be clearly understood.

When I learned I could convey different nuances of meaning by simply changing a few words, I was hooked! Simultaneously, the more proficient I became at wordsmithing, the more intelligent others viewed me. It wasn't long before I understood that my thoughts became clearer, more defined, and more achievable the more I was able to articulate them to myself.

I have discovered there is a serious link between one's ability to communicate effectively and the level of frustration they experience in a conversation. When a person is not able to find the right words, they may resort to doing other things to get their point across—or simply cursing, since F-bombs need no interpretation.

My personal definition of *frustration* is "an exasperated mind seeking desperately to find the right words to express itself." Nowhere is this more commonly seen than in relationships. When the right words cannot be found or recalled, the result is to withdraw or shut down in irritation. The conversation ends and the rift widens.

Sometimes people in a serious relationship forget that, more than ever before, they need to be watchful about the words that are spoken. Many people think they should *keep it real* with their spouse, especially in an argument, and just let the words fly. But the damage that can be done by speaking carelessly is astounding. Words are impossible to recapture once they've slipped out, and even a small or seemingly insignificant comment can cause massive destruction that lasts a lifetime.

Here is a practice I've found helpful: Pause before you speak.

Take a moment to say the words in your mind before they become public. This is a real challenge, but it may go far in averting unnecessary conflict. The task of speaking to your mate the way you want to be spoken to is not easy to achieve, though it's what we all want.

Many times during a heated exchange with my lovely wife— and we have had a few—I have to catch my breath and literally hold back what I want to say next. I ask myself, *Would I like to hear this spoken to me?* I'll try to play out the entire scenario of how she will respond if I continue with what I want to say. Often, my mental picture isn't pleasant. So I catch myself and intentionally change my words to something more satisfactory. Now, does that always work? Absolutely not! But more often than not, it does, and it also conveys the clear message that I'm respecting her with my words.

Also, it's better to do this early in the argument before things get too heated. When some couples are in the thick of the battle, they may be more willing to cross verbal boundaries. In fact, they may pause, think about what they are trying to say, realize that their intended words will be destructive and mean-spirited—and then say them anyway. Sometimes they will even freestyle mid-sentence to add extra venom and a few expletives. This type of communication can effectively close emotional doors to the point where the two individuals need serious counseling in order to reopen those doors again.

Guarding your words is an ongoing process. Do not give in or submit to defeat if you fail a few times and say some regrettable things. It takes effort, practice, and a serious appeal to your inner morality and decency to change your words. Without question, there will be slips and missteps, but the intent should always be to build up and not destroy. There should always be an underlying desire to speak positively to your mate, even if your words contradict that fact on occasion. Good intentions, a willing heart, and a positive effort can be a more powerful force for change and soften words over time.

Tone

The twin sibling to words is the tone with which they are given. A person can have the absolute perfect words to say, but the vehicle those words travel in might invalidate them completely before they even reach the listener. I have sat in front of many couples like Donnie and Kim and watched them struggle with trying to muster the right words. By the time those words actually come, they are packaged in a sarcastic covering that makes them offensive.

I'm a firm believer in the maxim "It's not so much what you say but how you say it." During one emotional breakthrough with a couple, I asked them to open up and simply apologize for the downward direction of their marriage. Even when coached, they both visibly struggled with saying the right thing. Then, when they finally found the correct thing to say, they were careless about their verbal packaging. So when that perfectly great apology ambled from their lips, it was presented in the most sarcastic and insincere manner—and therefore was ineffective.

I consider this a relationship phenomenon. We all know how we want to be talked to. We all respond so much better to kindness and sweetness. We all want to freely drink from the pleasant fountain of sweet vocal nectar that comes from the lips of our beloved mates. We want them to consider how we feel and what we need and carefully prepare their words so that we can hear the pleasantries with joy. Nevertheless, when the anger hits, we don't care two cents about how we respond to them.

Every discussion about an issue should begin with an even tone. Find your comfortable, conversational pitch and talk at that level. During the conversation, stay at that level even if you have to pause and consider how your voice sounds. I've even encouraged couples to ask each other, "Is my tone acceptable to you?" This will help you monitor how you are coming off to your mate. Once you both are comfortable, you will find it's acceptable to raise your voice when expressing a passionate point because your partner now knows you are cognizant of how you speak.

> We all want to freely drink from the pleasant fountain of sweet vocal nectar that comes from the lips of our beloved mates. We want them to consider how we feel and what we need and carefully prepare their words so that we can hear the pleasantries with joy. Nevertheless, when the anger hits, we don't care two cents about how we respond to them.

We are all emotional beings. We thrive on how something or someone *makes* us feel. When words are spoken, they connect with us intellectually. We know the meanings and understand the grammar of what was said. But that's not good enough. The tone, the inflection, and the intensity with which the message is given are what appeal to how we feel. They are what connect to our passion and our moods.

"I said I'm sorry!" may seem sincere coming from the offender, but there is seldom a way you can make that statement seem loving or sweet.

Gestures

Gestures are another communication pathway that may accompany our words. In order to communicate effectively, it is of the utmost importance for a presenter to be deliberate in what they do with their hands, posture, and neck. There is a stark difference between telling someone how you feel about what they did and pointing a finger in their face while you tell them how you feel. An aggressive gesture can elevate a conversation to an argument in seconds.

Raising hands is often seen as the precursor to a physical attack. I have sat in front of numerous individuals who *talk with their hands*. I have heard some say, "Well, that's just how I talk." My suggestion to them is to learn another language—one that does not include making aggressive gestures during a conversation.

When couples are in conflict, I often counsel them to keep their hands in their laps. They should lift their hands only if they are talking about themselves, not when talking about their mate. For instance, when a person puts their hand on their own chest to express hurt feelings, it's an effective way to convey deep and sensitive meaning. But when a person puts their finger on your chest to express hurt feelings, it doesn't convey to you a sense of being sensitive or understanding.

Similarly, one bad habit I've seen couples exhibit is pointing at each other when they talk, especially when angry. While it might seem like it's not a big deal to some, it can escalate an argument quickly. It can add fuel to an already volatile situation by injecting an element of intimidation. This and any other type of aggressive move such as raising the hand, lunging forward, or rhythmically clapping the hands with every angry word are all acts of aggression and will do nothing to subdue an argument.

The goal of conflict is understanding and resolution. This is easier said than done during the heat of the battle, but if both parties have this at the forefront of their minds, it's a start in the right direction.

> **The goal of conflict is understanding and resolution.**

Eyes

"The eyes are the windows to the soul." That's a common saying that has been attributed to many people but verified by none. It means your eyes can show your level of honesty or deceit.

As a child, I was often told by my elders to look at people in their eyes when talking to them. It shows honesty. But you don't have to be a scientist to know that emotions and true feelings are often shown through a person's eyes. In the middle of a conversation, you can tell if someone is listening or engaged simply by seeing whether their eyes are focused on you, or if their eyes are wandering. It is a telltale sign of whether a person is connecting with you.

Also, when you want to convey that you are not listening, it's easy to do so by rolling your eyes or raising your eyebrows. I have seen many couples pretend to listen when their spouse is talking, but their eyes are staring in a different direction. If you want to let your partner know you are engaged in what they're saying, make it known by how you look at them. A relaxed face and kind eyes will show that you are open enough to receive what is being said.

I must admit, this is one of my biggest challenges in communication. Depending on the level of absurdity of a comment, my eyes may take over in a moment, and before I know it, I'm fully engaged in eyebrow raising, squinting, and head shaking. But it all begins with the eyes. We have to remember that our eyes don't make decisions by themselves; they are controlled by the brain and the emotions. Whatever is in your heart, your eyes will reveal. So the key here is not to try and control your eyes, but rather control the way you're thinking and feeling about a particular situation—then your eyes will adjust.

> **Whatever is in your heart, your eyes will reveal. So the key here is not to try and control your eyes, but rather control the way you're thinking and feeling about a particular situation—then your eyes will adjust.**

Written Communication

I woke up abruptly one morning and turned to look over at my phone on the side table. Anxiety about an early meeting had prompted me to wake before the alarm sounded. As I picked up the phone, I saw I had missed a text from my twenty-year-old daughter, who was staying at her girlfriend's place for the evening.

The message simply said one word: "Accident."

Immediately sleepiness left me. I alerted my wife, and we called numerous times trying to reach our daughter. A hundred possible scenarios ran through my mind, each one worse than the last. She was in a terrible car accident and had the strength to type only one word. Or maybe she was in police custody and that was her one phone call. *It could be almost anything!* I thought as I went into panic mode.

Eventually, Wendy reached her as she groggily answered the phone.

"Hey, Mom, what's wrong?"

Wendy responded more calmly than I would have. "You texted Dad that you had an accident! What happened? Are you okay?"

"Huh?" she responded in confusion. "Oh! I dialed you by mistake at one thirty and then just texted you to let you know the call was an accident. I didn't want you to worry."

Mission not accomplished! We did worry. Her intent was to calm our fears, but her written communication left much to be desired in performing that noble task.

From the letters of yesteryear to the text messaging and DMs of today, written communication has never ceased. But unless you are a gifted poet, able to paint words on the canvas of another's soul, most people fall short in properly conveying their feelings through a memo. Often a person will choose to leave a written message as opposed to talking to their partner. While this may indeed avoid personal confrontation, it does very little to convey the actual message the writer desires.

Texts fall especially short in sharing negative emotions. Even emoticons don't accurately relay the proper feelings. The average person will find difficulty in expressing the sorrow and remorse of an apology through the written word. During the heat of a marital battle, a sentence expressing your discontent with a particular issue will more often than not be misconstrued by the reader. The writer's intention may be honest, but you can't truly read intentions. You can only read the black and white and then assume what you think the writer is trying to say.

Writing down how you feel may be beneficial to personally chronicle your emotions and sort out how your feel. This should be for personal use, just to organize your thoughts before you vocally share your heart. But because we read often through the lens of our own experiences and feelings, we may not get the true meaning of what another person is trying to convey through written communication. We get only our perceptions, and they fall short when trying to properly communicate.

Now, please don't think I'm saying you should never write a love letter to your partner. Of course you should! If the gist of the message is to share positive feelings of love, admiration, and passion, writing it will only leave room for improvement when the face-to-face communication takes place. You should write love letters or texts to your mate. Explore the passion and titillation of flirtation by writing a passionate letter to your love. This sets the stage for more endearing and constructive interactions when you come together.

Touch

When two people feel truly passionate toward one another, there is an innate desire to touch. We all have personal space that we want to protect when we communicate with another person. It's as though we have an invisible boundary we build around us, which serves as a warning to indicate whether we are in any danger or imminent peril. This is a natural and necessary thing.

When you meet a stranger, the first thing you do is to stand at a safe distance until you feel it's okay to approach. In fact, if you meet a stranger and that person immediately breaches your boundary and touches you—or even worse, hugs you—you may feel offended or at the very least put off by such unwelcome behavior. This is because we all value our personal safety and privacy.

Once you start to talk and have deep communication with someone, you may feel comfortable with having your personal space breached. In fact, if the attraction juices are really flowing, you may be the one to initiate it. The resulting touch will take your relationship to a different level.

When I first got married, I made it a practice that I would never go a day without significant physical touch with my wife. When we are in public, we automatically hold hands. It's a way of staying close and feeling connected. It also is a way we feel safe and protected.

Conversely, when there is a rift in the relationship, touch is the first thing that suffers. It's as though when there is conflict, we revert back to that personal safe space and erect those boundaries again. This is so we can't be hurt or so no one can come close. You see this mostly at night.

Kim and Donnie experienced this every night. She would go to her separate side of the bed, and he would do likewise. They refused to touch because doing so would mean becoming vulnerable. Someone would have to let down their guard. If they touched, they'd have to confront those resentful feelings because they would be sacrificing their safe spaces.

It is difficult to touch and not feel something. It may be a positive or a negative feeling, but touch will always elicit an emotion of some kind. It will always cause you to seriously confront whatever you're experiencing.

Now, when there is anger or pain in a relationship, you may

want to touch, but not for a positive reason. It is here that great caution and care must be taken. You can easily use touch in a negative way, perhaps to exact physical dominance or control. This, of course, is never advisable. In a relationship, touch should be supported only by positive feelings and affections.

The key here is to use touch in a way that draws your mate to you instead of driving them away.

Silence

When I coach couples through how to talk to each other, one of the main communication tools I use is silence. It is a very powerful thing to remain still and hushed while your partner is railing with anger. This isn't easy, but it is effective. What will invariably happen is that your partner will eventually run out of steam and ask you to respond.

This flies directly in the face of those who live by the maxim of fighting fire with fire. But I have never heard this proverb come from the mouth of a real firefighter, the overwhelming majority of whom would prefer to use water to douse raging conflagrations. Silence can be that water if used with an attentive and understanding gaze into your partner's eyes. On the other hand, silence can be fire if it is used to alienate.

For a person who wants to talk and thrives on vocal communication, intentional and spiteful silence can be just as offensive as negative words. At least with words, the person knows they are not being ignored. I have often seen frustrated spouses with tears welling in their eyes passionately beg their partner, "Just talk to me! Tell me what you're feeling!"

For the non-talker, this can feel like a time to exert power. They intentionally withhold information or feelings because they know that is exactly what their partner is craving. This is manipulation at its worst. The silent person, out of anger, is letting their spouse know they are not willing to engage. To the talker, it comes across as disrespectful and cruel, but they feel powerless, because barring painful types of torture, no one can force another person to talk. In this case, silence, which should be a mode of positive listening, becomes a powerful weapon to punish.

Pathways are used to achieve a specified result. When anyone travels a path, the expectation is to reach a desired destination. In marriage, the destination is to remove all barriers and impediments so that both parties can effectively understand and be understood. It is to create a safe landing place where your partner can know their innermost feelings are being respected and heard.

I have heard many individuals laud their own prowess at communicating, and then wonder why their relationship is in shambles. Generally, it's because a person can eloquently relay information so as to garner the praise of thousands, but that is not synonymous with intentionally and sensitively engaging another person's heart.

This is why the pathways are so necessary: showing an interest in what someone is saying by sincere eye contact; showing respect with a level tone; inviting safety by eliminating aggressive gestures; relaying sincerity with honest silence; and giving of your heart by well-chosen words. These are the ways necessary to create open and safe communication, and when intentionally implemented, these paths will save countless hours of needless pain and fruitless discussion.

Many couples feel that communication should just happen. It should be easy. This could not be further from the truth. For as complex and multifaceted as human beings are, there is no possible way we should all be able to simply relate without issue. And if you're going to pledge your life to another person in marriage, it is mandatory that you consider how important it is to study your mate and learn the best methods to relate.

CHAPTER 4

Punks Always Speak Their Mind

If there was one word you could use to describe Elena and Daniel's marriage, it would be *volcanic*. Their relationship has spewed the most toxic lava and ash for years, yet they still seem content to live inside the volcano. Every day there is a new challenge or unexpected conflict.

Danny was raised in Manhattan, New York. After emigrating, his old-country Italian grandparents fought hard to make a life for themselves and their six children at the family delicatessen in Little Italy. When they retired, they passed the successful Fine Eats Deli to their son and daughter-in-law, who, after thirty more years, passed it on to Danny.

On a daily basis, Danny would sling sharp-but-friendly insults and jabs at his regulars as they ordered their signature dishes. It was what he looked forward to; it was his life. After all, as a single man in New York, what could be better than food and fun?

This all changed one morning when Danny had his head down making his world-famous chicken parm hero during the lunch-time rush. He heard a lyrical voice speaking to the cashier.

"Excuse me, may I have an antipasto salad?" Elena was in a rush to get back to work.

Danny turned around and saw her—and that was the beginning of their story. He quickly told the cashier he'd ring this one up. Elena glanced at him. Even though she was rushing, she smirked at his obvious attraction.

"Um, will that be all, young lady...whom I've never seen before in my deli?" Danny was in full romance mode.

Her smirk broke into an all-out grin. "Yes, that will do it," she replied as she handed him the money for her meal.

"And here's your receipt!" When Elena looked down, she saw he had written his number on it.

"Do you give this to all your customers?"

Danny was intrigued by her quickness. "You're the absolute first...and last."

As Elena left the shop, they glanced at each other one last time. Danny confidently mouthed the words *Call me!*

Elena was not accustomed to someone being so forward. She had just moved to Manhattan from Toledo, Ohio, to work as a paralegal while she attended law school in the evenings, so her time was very precious to her. A relationship was the last thing she needed at that time.

Elena's father had died when she was young, and her mom had worked multiple jobs to make sure her two kids had all they needed. Elena was the older child and felt a responsibility to make good so her mom could finally relax and enjoy life. Besides, she wanted to set a good example for her younger sister. The pressure to succeed was real.

So calling Danny was completely out of her game plan. She didn't need any distractions.

Still, the fact that he seemed busy with his career might mean she didn't have to invest a great deal of time. And she really could use a weekend break from her grueling schedule. Besides, Danny was definitely cute. So she called.

They went out the following weekend, and all their expectations were realized. They joked and sarcastically prodded each other and laughed continuously. This was more than either of them could have asked for. They saw each other during lunch hours when Elena came almost daily to pick up her food and chat for a few minutes. It was a perfect setup.

Eighteen months later, Elena had completed law school, advanced from paralegal to associate attorney, and was planning a wedding. She and Danny were smitten with each other. Their joking, sarcasm, and banter had become a staple in their relationship. It all seemed fun—until it wasn't anymore.

After five years, Elena felt a child, a new home, and burgeoning careers required a different type of communication. She didn't like that her son was starting to be just as sarcastic as his father. She wanted more depth and heart rather than banter and cynicism. Elena needed help. She needed a deeper, kinder way of communication. She wanted to feel more value and respect as opposed to the kind of harsh teasing they had become so accustomed to. But when she expressed this to Danny, he simply brushed it off with his usual sardonic commentary.

Their relationship had become such that even when friends

came over, they had to have thick skin to survive. Communication in their house was never a problem. *How* they communicated was a completely different story. Light sarcasm and jovial teasing had slowly turned into mean-spirited joking. They had settled into a very bad habit of satirical conversation.

Because they didn't reach any emotional depth, Danny and Elena started to be callous in their interactions; nothing was really off-limits to criticize. Their arguments became more frequent and seemingly crueler. Every now and then there came a glimpse of depth and heart, but then it was back to the unkind joking and fending off real emotions. They were in a bad place and were losing hope. All they knew was that they didn't like the way they conversed and they couldn't sustain this disconnect much longer. They needed help to survive.

PRACTICE MAKES PERFECT

There is a myth that once you are married, you should be free to speak your mind. While there is a measure of truth to this, there is also a marital decorum that should be observed with your mate. That doesn't mean you should tolerate an uncomfortable environment, or that people can't *be themselves*. But it does mean if you want to have open and vulnerable communication, you'll need to make a deliberate effort to do so, which may seem sometimes unnatural and rehearsed. And that is perfectly okay! The idea that everything has to flow naturally in a relationship is another myth.

In every difficult pursuit—and marriage is near the top of the list—you must practice important skills before they become natural. It's like swimming, which I personally still have to perfect. While some may paddle around naturally, for those of us who sink like a boulder, it takes intentional and mostly unnatural arm movements, hand cupping, and proper leg paddling to keep from sinking and actually make forward progress.

The same dogged persistence has to be understood and achieved in communicating. None of this just happens naturally. You have to recondition yourself away from bad habits and actually pay attention to how you are interacting with your mate. This may seem awkward and abnormal, but the goal is to be effective and refine your ability to communicate with your partner.

I believe everyone has a right to be talked to in the way they choose to be talked to. In other words, we all know how we want to be addressed. There is a comfort level when it comes to tone, pitch, gestures, and word usage that will elicit the best responses from us. I often put it this way: "I can't tell you how to talk to anyone else, but this is how you're going to talk to me if you want a reasonable response."

Years ago, during one of my earliest pastoral experiences, I was engaged in a heated conversation with an irate church member. As a young twenty-something pastor, I was flustered and didn't respond well. Watching from the sideline was an elderly gentleman whom I greatly admired for his insight and humor. He pulled me to the side after the skirmish and imparted some wisdom that has stuck with me to this day.

He simply said, "Pastor," and then he paused for comedic effect, "it is possible to tell somebody to *go to hell* in such a way that they will think about it and say, 'Okay, that's a good idea.'" What he meant is *how* you present your thoughts and ideas is critical as to whether the hearer will accept them.

There are three approaches we can take when we talk to another person. These are the essential ways we communicate, and understanding each approach will increase the likelihood of receiving a hoped-for response.

TALKING AT

Let's begin with the most unproductive way to speak to anyone: *talking at* a person. Just by mentioning that phrase, I'm sure you can already relate to what it means. This is the most careless way to communicate to another person and often results in confrontation. Talking at a person assumes, to the hearer, that they are your inferior or are at a lower state than you.

It is akin to speaking as though that person does not have the capacity to understand adult communication. I've often seen this happen when one spouse does not respect the other person's opinion or they may be so heated that, at the time, getting their point across is the most important thing. Irrespective of the circumstances surrounding talking at your spouse, it always comes across as disrespectful and dismissive.

For the sake of argument, let's look at any positive sides to talking at your mate. The only positive that comes to mind has to be the intention. In some cases, when a person is speaking at their spouse, there is an intention of instructing that person and giving them information that will better them. They are trying to make a possibly valid point, but the delivery is hiding the intent and hindering any weight the message may carry. Most people who talk at others may not even feel they are superior, but when anger takes over and the primary goal is to make a point, *talking at* becomes involuntary. This is where Elena and Danny had settled.

My wife, Wendy, and I had been married only a few months when we had our first big argument. Because of her hot Caribbean blood and my *never-back-down* Southern upbringing, it was a doozie! She came in hot, complete with finger pointing and high-volume, *talking at* me as if I were a child or her inferior. Well, that immediately triggered a response and I returned fire while dodging perfectly aimed verbal missiles. It wasn't pretty, but it was necessary. I expressed to her just how hurtful it was to be *talked at*, sharing that it is something you do to an unruly pet, not a human being. She understood and we reconciled, but the story didn't end there.

Some weeks later, after we were now all cozy and in a good place, the situation reversed itself and I spoke at her as though she were a child. World War Two began! But this time we understood what was happening. The missiles were not as big and the aim was not as direct—because we recognized the kind of damage that could be caused by carelessly speaking at each other.

Wendy and I learned we had to clearly define how we wanted to be communicated with and being talked at was definitely out of the question. In her past, Wendy had experienced relationships where she was spoken to very negatively. This caused her to detest being spoken to in that manner, as if she were inferior. However, the corollary to that was that she learned to speak that way to others. I had also been subjected to negative communication and comments; as a result, those habits became weapons in my arsenal.

This is an unfortunate truth: Often the verbal poison that has been thrown at us becomes the same venom we spew at others, all the while despising what we're doing.

I call this *destructive criticism*. There is no real benefit to talking at someone. Even our pets will tuck their tails between their legs and run away when they hear that negative tone. The only result of this type of communication is emotional pain. Even if the speaker may not intend to cause distress, and even if he or she is trying to get a valid point across, simply because of the arrangement of their words, their tone, and the intensity of the message, the hearer may be completely put off.

As a side note, many parents have gotten into the habit of talking at their children. Growing up, I remember hearing quite a few sayings that weren't meant to be demeaning, but nevertheless made me feel small:

- "You don't speak till you are spoken to!"
- "Children are to be seen and not heard!"
- "What's wrong with you?"
- "Shut up before I beat you!"

I'm sure you can insert many other sayings you have either heard or used. This can be a hard lesson for parents to learn, but children need to feel as though they are equal in value even though we understand they are not equal in function or responsibility.

Now, you may ask, "How do I even know if I'm talking at someone? What if they are just being overly sensitive?"

The only sure way to know is to observe the listener. People are not androids. We all have feelings and emotions we share. If a person is insulted because of how you speak to them, they will respond accordingly by shutting down or firing back at you. You may not even be aware of your tone or how you are phrasing your comments in a negative way. But if you are the one never invited to the office parties and you know your hygiene is good, it may be because your communication needs an overhaul.

What's the solution to spouses who "talk at" each other? It starts by asking your partner, "How would you like to be spoken to?" Yes, it's awkward. It's unnatural. But doing so starts the conversation and avoids breakdowns in what could be a rewarding relationship.

You will never truly know how to effectively communicate with your mate until you ask them what they need. It's simple but true.

> You will never truly know how to effectively communicate with your mate until you ask them what they need. It's simple but true.

TALKING TO

Now, let's discuss *talking to* your mate. This is where most of us live. Let's call it the default mode of communication.

We talk to our spouses about how our days went. We talk to our dates about their lives so we can get to know them better. We will talk to coworkers and other colleagues about projects and initiatives that need to be implemented. We even talk to strangers about the weather or about their cute puppy romping around at the park. This is the most common way to communicate. I have spent countless hours in classrooms where instructors have droned on about theology or psychology. Teachers or mentors talk to us to give us information. It is mostly an instructive way of speaking and is all about broadcasting information and getting feedback.

While the idea of *talking to* may seem like I'm picking at semantics—especially in a marriage book—that couldn't be further from the truth. The way in which you communicate with people on a daily basis cannot be the exclusive way you speak to your spouse.

That was the problem with Elena and Danny. Home

communication was no different than conversations with friends, coworkers, or strangers. The same line of questioning and the same uninspiring answers. They didn't know how to get beyond the emotional roadblocks they had created. They were like a number of couples who have become careless in attending to their relationship and doing the work necessary to go emotionally deeper. As a result, they remain in this uninspiring space of speaking to each other about things, places, and events that neither of them truly cares about.

I have known couples who have stayed together for decades and never got beyond just talking to their mate. They endure lives together, and though they may not be as volatile as Elena and Danny, they will enjoy only a moderate level of depth in their relationship. They speak kindly to each other and may even be respectful toward each other, but they experience a level of sameness that can be frustrating.

Here's a clarification: *Talking to* your mate is not a bad way to communicate. We all do this on a daily basis, and it is necessary to move along and get things done. However, it's not a sustainable state of existence for people who want deeper connections. Couples need to push through this phase in order to find that depth.

Unfortunately, when couples get stuck on this level, they can become extremely bored. One spouse may even start an argument just to do something different. They long for a passionate exchange in some form—any form! And if there is never any attempt to dive into more meaningful conversations, they may look elsewhere to meet that emotional need.

When I've spoken to couples who have had affairs, this seems to be a recurring theme. A lonely wife or a bored husband just needed someone to listen to them and understand. They missed the passion and the emotion they used to have with their spouse. They are tired of being treated like a roommate.

While none of these are acceptable reasons for anyone to have an emotional or physical affair, the truth still can't be denied. Communication takes thought and work. Couples must dig beneath the surface and have earnest conversations about their feelings and emotions. Humans cannot be emotionally healthy without connecting on this level.

TALKING WITH

This brings us to the most transformative way to communicate, and that is *talking with* your partner. When a person does this, they are actually communicating feelings and emotions, not just facts and events. When you talk *with*, there is a mutual understanding and an emotional connection. You don't just speak with your mate; you feel what they are saying.

Elena and Danny never got to this level because they had erected barriers to intimacy early in their relationship. The sarcastic banter and rough teasing created an environment where it wasn't easy to reveal sensitive emotions and vulnerability for fear of being attacked. They both wanted to speak at that level, but it was difficult to trust that the other person would honor the other one's openness and handle their feelings carefully.

While I believe wholeheartedly that the ability to laugh and even joke is healthy in a relationship, there must be boundaries. There has to be a mutual understanding that sometimes, when you're pouring your heart out because you really need to be heard and understood, joking is simply not welcome. There is a time and a place for levity and even light sarcasm, but when people are emotionally exposed is not that time.

When there is a mutual engagement and trust, closeness and a deeper appreciation for your mate is inevitable. But it takes time and consistency to reverse bad habits. Elena and Danny will have to force themselves to monitor how and when they engage in banter and when it's time to be serious. As I said earlier, this may be awkward and unnatural, but the road to relationship wellness is not covered with gum drops and candy canes with rainbows above. There must be intentional effort to notice when you are not emotionally reaching your mate, and then to humbly ask questions as to what you're doing that's blocking the road to recovery.

When you are talking with your partner and they feel as though they are actually being heard and cared about, even the criticism will be constructive. It will actually get through and they will be more apt to listen because they understand it's coming from a sincere and honest place. This is the essence of *constructive criticism*. It builds and makes a person better.

Let's say Danny wants to tell Elena his heart. It might go something like this:

"Hey, Lena, got a minute?" he begins as he jokingly plops his 200-pound frame on the side of the bed.

She sighs deeply as she jolts from the bed, shaking. Expecting the worst, she gently rubs her temple and ekes out her response. "Sure…what is it?"

He quickly spouts, "Well, dang! What's up with the attitude? I didn't say anything yet! I'm not gonna ask you for a kidney!"

She fakes a smile and then, obviously annoyed, asks slowly but deliberately, "What do you want, Danny?"

Now, Danny had every intention of being open and honest. He wanted a moment of vulnerability. This was his chance to push through her warranted frustration, break through the emotional barrier, and simply tell her his heart. After all, he jokes so much, why would she expect anything different this time? So as of right now, he can turn the conversation in any direction he chooses.

He can *talk at* her and berate her attitude with destructive criticism. He can tell her how he was gonna say something nice, but she doesn't deserve it because of her nasty attitude. He can *talk to* her and keep the conversation at a safe level by talking about the kids, work, or school. He can talk about tomorrow's agenda, which will only give her information and instructions without reaching deeper. Or he can finally push past his own insecurities and fears and trust that she wants deeper, more meaningful conversations and finally begin to talk with her. Let's say he chooses the latter. Here's how the scenario should go.

Danny stands up and walks around to Lena's side of the bed. Every impulse inside him is telling him to just walk away since she is giving no acknowledgment that he even exists. She is cold and rigid, refusing to even look at him.

He stands there for a moment and gathers his thoughts. He forces himself to soften his facial features and then sits down gently and takes her unresponsive hand. He looks in her eyes for a moment, all the while pushing through his own reluctance. He pushes past her frustration and weak attempt to pull her hand away and holds on tighter. He then takes a cleansing breath and he says in his most calm and sincere tone:

"Lena, honey. I love you. I really do," and he keeps eye contact with her, even though she's not returning the gaze. "I want you to feel safe to talk to me. It hurts me to see the sadness in your eyes;

that you don't trust me with your heart. I want to be your protector and your safe place to land. Up to this point, I know I've fallen short."

She rolls her eyes in frustration, but he pushes past it and continues. "I know I can be a better man for you; a more caring and patient person. Let me know when I'm not living up to what you expect, and I'll listen; I promise you. I'll do whatever it takes to create an environment where you can feel secure and loved and I will always love you like you deserve to be loved."

He then pauses quietly and waits for a response. He has just opened the door wide so that she can feel safe to enter. No joking. No sarcasm. No cynical expressions; just an open heart sincerely waiting for her. Now the onus is on her to accept his olive branch so they can start moving in a different direction.

Even if she can't respond fully and emotionally at that time, she should return his emotion with a tighter grip of his hand. Or she may soften her posture. Anything to indicate that she has heard him, even if she is not ready to respond.

This is where things can either move forward or fall apart. If Danny jumps up in frustration and says, "I tried and you're sitting there like you don't even care!" then his entire offer will be seen as insincere or just a tactic. Even if she does not respond, he should simply affectionately touch her hand or kiss her on the cheek and then walk away slowly, giving her time to process what just happened. The goal here is to resolve issues and not fuel them; to provide an opening where your spouse can feel safe to enter and be heard.

This is the difference between talking at, talking to, and talking with. So let's recap.

Talking at:

- Occurs when speaking to a subordinate or someone you feel is less than you.
- Is more concerned with getting the point across than with the feelings of the hearer.
- Does not care about gestures, pitch, tone, or respect.
- Uses destructive criticism and doesn't show value for the other person's opinion.

Talking to:

- Is general communication as with a stranger. Comfortable talking about events and facts.
- Is informational. Gives instructional criticism, directions, etc.
- Maintains a safe level of communication that refrains from going emotionally deep.

Talking with:

- Is characterized by patience with the other person's responses and is not argumentative.
- Asks sincere, vulnerable questions to find out sincere, open answers.
- Is not concerned with who is right but is willing to accept responsibility.
- Though passionate, does not show intense anger or disrespect.
- Is willing to hear and accept whatever is in the heart of the other person.

CHAPTER 5

Punks Don't Know How to Argue

Violet and Harvey were two of the most toxic people I have ever met, even though they chose to stay married for twenty-eight years. You would have to know them personally not to think they were sworn enemies. I met them at a social gathering of couples. It was a pleasant evening with dinner, polite conversation, and music. But after a couple glasses of wine, one real beast emerged—and his name was Harvey.

The argument I witnessed that evening was one for the ages. It felt as though I was ringside at a poorly matched heavyweight boxing championship. Except at this bout, the gloves were off, there were no rules, and you could only win by knockout.

I was aghast as I witnessed a lively and fun debate about relationships devolve into a personal fecal festival between two married people. There were personal shots, name calling, and just plain nasty insults. Sadly, as everyone else became awkwardly silent and pretty much afraid to comment, you could tell this was not unusual for Violet and Harvey. They seemed accustomed to ignoring the obvious social cues and going for the jugular.

Usually, I dare not pass judgment on a marriage without knowing the history or backstory. However, you don't have to take the pulse of roadkill. It was pretty obvious the end had already come for Violet and Harvey; they were just lying in the road—or worse, still running over each other.

ARGUING IS NOT THE PROBLEM

While I haven't met many couples who actually enjoy intense and heated arguing, there is a place for argument and debate in every relationship. When arguing gets out of hand, however, things can become destructive very quickly.

Here is the straight truth: Arguing is not the problem. Arguing is not necessarily an indicator of a bad or dying relationship. It simply shows there is conflict that needs to be resolved by passionate and concerned people. Debating in a marriage is just two people trying to get their points across in the hope that they will be listened to and understood. The key is that there must be a mutual regard for one another's value.

When most people come to an argument, they are passionate about what they believe and usually just want their views to be heard and understood. They have an idea or opinion that may or may not have any real foundation—but it's their idea, and they feel it should be given fair attention.

There are many ways they try to make their opinion heard. They look for holes in their opponent's argument. They will try to invalidate points with their own set of facts. They will seize upon moments when they can get their rival emotionally charged or thrown off their game, so as to prove to them the folly of their argument. They will use passive-aggressive arguments—or in some cases, name calling—when frustration reaches a high level.

These may all be effective techniques in a courtroom or on a debate team. But when it comes to a relationship where two people have committed to each other, there must be a finer line to walk. It is never advisable to do away with all civility and decorum and just let the words fly without any consideration as to where or how they land. There must be a balance between fully expressing your opinion and still maintaining respect for your partner.

My goal when talking to couples in conflict is to get them to see the value in having conflicting opinions. Contrary to what many think, it's actually beneficial to disagree on a number of issues. If a couple always thinks the same and has the same viewpoints, they will never learn from each other. But when their opinions diverge, it becomes an opportunity to grow and increase understanding.

I often find it refreshing to hear opposite views to mine. It allows me to gain perspective and grow intellectually from observing someone else's vantage point.

I once heard a young woman brag that she never heard her parents argue and she wants that kind of marriage. While I understand her desire to live a life without conflict, it's very unreasonable. What she was missing was that she never had a positive role model of how to resolve conflict. She never saw her parents argue, disagree, and then make up. This is what is normal and what children need to see. They need to see parents who know how to get through the rough times but do so with respect and poise. She only saw them suppress and never engage in differences of opinion.

Again, arguing is not the problem. It's arguing incorrectly that causes all the damage.

GROWTH AND CHANGE ARE NOT THE PROBLEM

Think of it this way: Arguing and resolving conflict is the fertilizer that nourishes the relationship, so growth can take place. Fertilizer contains waste and debris that may not seem pleasant or fragrant, but it is necessary for people to thrive, because the only evidence of life is growth.

As individuals, we are constantly growing and changing. Just because two people choose to marry and become one, it doesn't mean they lose their individuality. They still have personal goals and personal growth. We are not the same people we were twelve months, six months, or even a week ago. In fact, we grow by the moment. We all change and have different goals, thoughts, and aspirations.

Now, as we grow individually, we also grow as couples through shared experiences. These two paths of growth can happen concurrently. Personal and communal growth within a marriage does not need to be a problem. In fact, it should be a sign of health!

The key is to come together and notify each other when you have changed, and to communicate about what is different in the present. It's necessary to talk about how your individual growth is influencing your mutual growth.

For example, a wife may have enjoyed her husband bringing

her roses or cooking her favorite meal for the last five years, but now she's wearied of it. He may have enjoyed a neck rub or that one sexy outfit she wears, but now his tastes have changed. These things need to be discussed because people are constantly growing and changing. Notification of these changes is only logical.

However, the straight truth is that most of us don't do that. Instead, most people simply allow these changes to happen and then argue about how things are different. *You're not the same person you used to be.* Of course not! Who is?

This discipline of connecting to notify each other of how you've changed requires constant communication. Sadly, many couples feel this is too much to talk about. They think their partner should just notice the changes. *If you really loved me, you would see that I'm different now and you'd know what I need.* Of course, such reasoning is ridiculous. It's not fair or logical to expect your spouse to spend all their waking hours watching to see how you have evolved. This is what communication is for. It's a time to reveal who you are and who you are becoming.

HOW TO GROW TOGETHER

Now here's the challenge: When a couple comes together, there will be rough edges recently created because of individual growth. Think of it this way: Each new like or dislike, each new idea or personal development, is an imaginary edge that you have grown. So we all have multiple little protrusions that are sticking out of our personalities. Again, these are natural and expected, and the longer you live, the more you will acquire. A new college degree, a new perspective on politics, a change in values are all new projections in your personality.

Coming together as a couple and talking about those edges or changes, and then working to find similarities, is where real relationship growth takes place. When you discuss these modifications in your personality, the goal is to smooth off the rough edges and find mutual uniformity. This is how two people grow together and actually enjoy the changes in each other.

Some protrusions may fit together perfectly with your partner, who is also changing. This is a beautiful thing when you find that you both are changing together and fitting together wonderfully. This will happen a lot of times. But then there are the other edges that don't fit. These sharp differences may irritate your partner, which is where arguments happen. This is where conflict arises. All of a sudden no one is thinking about the similarities, because the focus is on the areas that don't agree.

> **The goal in these moments is to work on the rough patches until you can find places that don't hurt; places that are comfortable.**

The goal in these moments is to work on the rough patches until you can find places that don't hurt; places that are comfortable.

Change is inevitable. There is nothing you can do to keep it from happening. Your partner will be different next year. So will you. But how you handle those differences is the key. Being able to talk about what you don't like anymore or how your opinions have changed—and still respect the fact that your spouse may not have changed in that same area—is a sure sign of maturity. It shows that you respect your mate's intellect and their ability to be different from you, and you love that about them.

Some feel that as soon as they have a disagreement, there is a problem. I've had many couples tell me that they argue all the time. I normally will respond, "Great! That means you're talking." There is still passion and a desire to express your feelings.

Let me add here that it's important to rush to reconcile your issues. It makes no difference where the issue originated or who you feel is to blame. The moment either of you senses a legitimate challenge to your relationship, be the first to talk about it. Never just wait for resolution to appear, because then you've allowed opinions to occur that may be completely wrong about the actual concern. Instead, approach problems quickly, when they're first seen, and resolve them before they can fester.

Remember this: Ten minutes of preemptive discussion about an issue can save you ten days of unnecessary tension and conflict.

> **Remember this: Ten minutes of preemptive discussion about an issue can save you ten days of unnecessary tension and conflict.**

I'm always excited to hear that a couple is arguing. It means all they need is direction, because they are already opening up and ready to say what's in their hearts. They are tired of being silent and want to get their points across. The need to express and be understood is necessary to find solutions to any challenge. It is the starting point.

Back to our argumentative couple. Harvey didn't realize Violet had changed. Then again, I don't think he realized much about what was happening around him. In a conversation with their friend, I found out Violet had been much more passive when they were first married. She basically let Harvey take the lead and be *the man*. He was the breadwinner and she stayed home—but she didn't just vegetate there. Instead, she took great advantage of her free time and went back to college. She earned her degree and became a very proficient accountant with a big firm.

Harvey, on the other hand, continued in his same position. They never had children, although they wanted to; it just didn't happen for them. They were both saddened by that but never gave it much conversation. They just poured themselves into their careers.

Violet found her voice and her respect from her work. Harvey felt left behind since she now earned a greater income. They never came together to smooth the rough edges. They continued being married because she felt obligated given that he'd paid for her education; besides, he was the only family she had. He blamed her for their not having a family. So their arguments were a way of expressing their anger and frustrations. They didn't fight fair because they didn't feel that life was fair.

Fortunately, for those who are not as severe as Violet and Harvey, there is a way to argue positively and with purpose.

DEALING WITH DESTRUCTIVE EMOTIONS

The most difficult part of arguing is having to deal with one's own pride. In a lot of ways, pride is a good thing. To feel good about yourself and to congratulate your own accomplishments is positive and healthy. Pride becomes a problem when it masquerades as stubbornness and arrogance, which is only a step away from anger and disrespect. And this is the emotion that rears its ugly head in most heated arguments.

Harvey had never checked his own pride at the door. Therefore, he lived a life of anger in regard to his wife. He was angry about his own lack of success in comparison to hers. He was angry that she now had a voice and a career, and he felt the only way to protect his own feelings of self-worth was to tear her down. She consequently learned to return the insults in order to protect herself from feeling defeated.

Anger is never pretty. It is seldom useful in resolving an argument or a debate. When a person becomes angry, they have actually lost their ability to think clearly and reasonably. Health is compromised, and decisions are made that are later regretted.

One Harvard University study observed how anger can affect the heart. "Although the risk of experiencing an acute cardiovascular event with any single outburst of anger is relatively low, the risk can accumulate for people with frequent episodes of anger," explained Dr. Elizabeth Mostofsky, an instructor in the department of epidemiology at the Harvard T.H. Chan School of Public Health. But you don't need a medical degree to know personally what happens when a person blows their top. Their heart speeds up, they feel intense heat, detach from reality, and basically lose it.

At the point when a couple such as Violet and Harvey are intensely arguing, they lose all decorum and social awareness. They are no longer concerned about what people think. The only thing that concerns them is causing another person harm or injury. They are in attack mode and all bets are off. I've seen couples who were lovey-dovey at one session, but then showed up for the next one armed and ready to destroy.

What causes this change in personality? What happened to all the love?

The answer is, it's all about protecting your heart. We know the power of anger. We know it's intimidating and scary, so we use it to intimidate and scare. It's a way of breaking people down and getting them to comply. Whether we do it consciously or out of sheer uncontrolled rage, the object is the same: to destroy.

Now, I need to point out the difference between hurtful anger and what I call righteous indignation. To be legitimately angry because of an injustice is normal. If you become angry in defense of a loved one or to right a wrong, that is noble and that cannot be compared to rage. That kind of wrath dissipates when the objective is accomplished, your loved one is safe, or the vulnerable party is adequately defended. But if the rage continues after the noble gesture has been made, it will morph into something destructive.

In relationship conflict, I have seen anger spouted out in vitriolic adjectives and venomous nouns. Or at extreme levels, it can become physical when people actually cross personal boundaries and attempt to exercise bodily dominance over their mate. When this happens, there needs to be immediate separation until the situation can be brought under control. While I've had many couples who have fought and stayed together, it takes a serious and intentional change of heart and behavior before I would ever advise this.

Some anger issues may require professional intervention. They may be the result of suppressed emotional hurt or unresolved pain. For some who have been around anger and repressed feelings all their lives, reacting aggressively is as common as breathing. Confronting the root of the issue is the first step.

HOW TO FIGHT FAIR

Now let's talk about fighting fair. Again, I believe it is healthy to argue and have different opinions, but there are rules to doing it with success. Specifically, you need to argue with positivity and purpose. If an argument doesn't lead to a greater understanding of your mate and a resulting closeness, then you are really terrible at arguing, just as Harvey and Violet were.

Create Boundaries

The first rule of fair fighting is to create and observe boundaries. There must be some parameters that you and your spouse adhere to when arguing.

There are millions of thoughts that run through your mind in the heat of battle. Mainly because the goal is to win the argument. But when arguing with your mate, winning is not the goal—resolution is. Consequently, never go for the jugular and bring up issues you know are personal and sensitive and could cause lasting damage in the relationship. That's an important boundary.

We all know what our mates' sensitivities are. We know the deeply personal issues we've shared during intimate times. Those issues are to be valued and are never to be brought into battle, even when you're losing the fight. Though the temptation may be strong to reach back and pull out one of these weapons, the damage caused by doing so will far outweigh any satisfaction gained by winning the argument. We will discuss this more in later chapters.

Remember, you are trying to resolve an issue, not create a world war. Which brings me to the next rule.

Seek Resolution

The second rule of fair fighting is to argue with resolution in mind. Each individual has to ask themselves this question during a dispute: *What is the goal?* If the goal is to win or to just make a point because you want to be heard, then don't engage when you're heated. Because if you want to be heard, arguing with an angry person won't accomplish that.

Hopefully the answer to the question is that you want to resolve the issue. Always have the goal of agreement in mind. If, at the onset of the discussion, you both can agree that you're going to discuss this concern and look for unity or agreement, then it takes the sting out of the conflict and gives it purpose. When people know there is no ill intent or that they won't be personally attacked, it becomes easier to debate the issue with unity of purpose.

Be Genuine

Another rule is to be genuine. This means arguing for a resolution is not the time to be passive-aggressive, which is when a person indirectly expresses negative feelings instead of directly addressing them. The purpose of this type of debating is to prove the point without taking full responsibility for the conflict, which can be seen as manipulative or insincere. It is a very frustrating way to discuss any topic, and in many instances will cause the other person to experience immediate annoyance if they don't shut down completely.

A close cousin of passive-aggression is mean sarcasm. This is a form of mocking and is used to create distance in an emotional discourse. Some believe the kind of irony expressed in sarcasm is supposed to make a point or reveal some deeper reality. I think sarcasm is detrimental to openness and does not lead to resolution;

rather, it perpetuates the problem in many cases. If you are serious about coming to some kind of mutually beneficial conclusion, making a sarcastic joke or a mean-spirited comment is not the way to do it.

Identify the Problem

The next rule of fair fighting is to objectify the problem. This is quite different from objectifying a person, which is totally unacceptable in any social setting. But literally, the word means to bring something to the status of a mere object. While this should never be done with people, it is necessary to do it with marital discord, so the problem can be minimized to a thing and not attached to a person.

Take the challenge and externalize it, so you both can objectively look at it from all sides. Then treat the problem like it's a task to be handled and not a larger-than-life issue. Imagine the issue as an enemy of the marriage that both parties must join together to attack.

Now, this is where a lot of couples miss the mark. They find it difficult to isolate the problem because they believe the person they are arguing with is the actual culprit. But as difficult as this might be, you must disconnect the problem from the person. By doing this, you will be able to find a resolution that does not involve discarding the person who initiated the conflict.

I often tell couples to identify the problem and then write it down if necessary. Verbalize it. Then put it on an imaginary shelf as if it were an actual object. That issue you've identified is the problem, not your spouse. Your spouse is a human being with many frailties and faults, just as you are. They make mistakes and have regrets. We all do and we all want to be understood and given the grace to be wrong.

Once the problem has been sufficiently secluded and set in a place where you both can look at it, then you both can discuss how to tackle it. You both can offer an opinion of the problem without anyone feeling personally attacked.

Harvey and Violet could have benefitted from objectifying their issues. The fact that he felt like he was being left behind in the marriage and that he was frustrated with his own life should have been something they both could have shelved. They could then talk about what was needed to help him find purpose and also why he chose to take his frustration out on Violet.

She in turn could have isolated the fact that she felt disrespected and that she wanted her voice back. They could have talked about the issues as though they were talking about a third party. They could have objectively discussed these sensitive topics without personal feelings getting involved.

Now, I know this seems like an almost impossible task and seldom have I seen couples perfect the usage of this technique. It takes time, sometimes years, to detach the issues from your partner. But marriage is supposed to be for a lifetime anyway. And objectifying issues may take years of hard work, trial, and failure. But nothing I talk about in this book is a quick fix. I don't believe in quick fixes or temporary patches. This is a lifelong venture.

End the Conflict

The final rule of fair fighting is to actively and intentionally end the conflict once a resolution has been reached.

People often have difficulty letting things go, and that's certainly true within a marriage. Someone may bring up an old conflict, days or weeks later, which creates a trigger. Though objectifying the issue will help resolve it, I advise couples to clearly define when the argument has ended. By the way, you won't find that resolution if you utter those infamous words "I'm fine." Here's a news flash. That never works!

There are two ways to successfully end a conflict. You can either call a truce or reach a compromise.

A truce is an agreement that you and your spouse are not going to argue anymore over an issue. This has to have mutual buy-in and an understanding that fighting over the problem isn't benefiting either of you. This is the same as agreeing to disagree. It's making a formal acknowledgment that you both have different opinions on an issue, and it is perfectly fine if you don't agree.

As intelligent individuals with different points of view, you can reasonably expect that issues will arise where there is not complete agreement. After all, you are not the same person. But a truce says that you value each other too much to let any disagreement destroy your relationship. The marriage is more important than the problem, so you will respect the different viewpoints you both bring and will leave it at that. The issue may not be agreed upon, but the fact that you can both respect and accept each other's differences is the resolution.

For example, a couple may have different political views. One may be conservative, while another favors more liberal views. These may be long-standing opinions that existed before the individuals met each other. However, they have found that their relationship is bigger than politics. So they may occasionally engage in light banter, but they realize there's a truce in place that says they will never let their differences in opinion destroy their marriage. The truce is that they have resolved to live and respect their differences.

The other way to end a conflict is through a compromise. With a compromise, both parties have to give in or surrender their opinion (or a part of that opinion) to the other person. This is more difficult than a truce because it may feel as though there's a winner and a loser. But it's not about wins and losses; it's about resolution, especially when both are giving something away for the greater good.

> Compromise is the stuff that great marriages are made of. Giving up one's pride to gain peace is really the best bargain you could ever broker in any discussion.

Compromise is the stuff that great marriages are made of. Giving up one's pride to gain peace is really the best bargain you could ever broker in any discussion. It's not always necessary to have the last word, as long as there is mutual respect and you both understand that there is shared sacrifice. With a compromise, both parties walk away feeling as though they are winners, because the relationship has won.

The way to determine if you've actually resolved the battle is when both parties can end the discussion feeling good about their spouse. If there are lingering negative feelings, then it's not over yet. You will have to revisit the issue, maybe later, so that you both can have a sense of peace.

Arguing is a necessary evil. But the bite is significantly reduced when a couple has the tools to do it effectively. It is vital to remember that conflict has a purpose and there are rules to effective arguing. And that healthy growth can occur when a couple puts time and intentional effort into finding resolution.

This is not an easy thing to do. Marriage is not a microwave proposition; it's a slow-cooker recipe that requires multiple ingredients and may takes years to complete. But those who last through the triumphs and failures are the ones who enjoy the spoils.

> Marriage is not a microwave proposition; it's a slow-cooker recipe that requires multiple ingredients and may take years to complete. But those who last through the triumphs and failures are the ones who enjoy the spoils.

CHAPTER 6

Punks Are Afraid to Get Naked

Candace, her parents, and her brother-in-law were all huddled in the birthing room, anxious to witness her sister Shani's first delivery. It was an exciting time for everyone there. This was the first grandchild in the family. Her sister did not want anyone to know the gender until she delivered.

Everything was going great. Contractions were now about three minutes apart, and Shani was starting to panic a little because of the intense pain.

"Maybe we should call Dr. Z," Shani said as she smirked at Candace.

Dr. Z was the man Shani had been bragging about to Candace ever since her first visit to her new ob-gyn. Candace was so focused on her career as a morning news producer that she didn't take time to date. Shani always looked out for her little sister and felt Dr. Zion Carter was someone she should meet.

As another contraction hit, Shani screamed just as the much-talked-about doctor walked in the door.

"Hey, Shani," he said lightheartedly, "don't scream in excitement just because I'm here!" Everyone chuckled as he introduced himself.

Candace forgot all about the delivery and caught herself staring at Dr. Z. He, of course, couldn't help noticing how beautiful she was. Shani was absolutely correct. Their chemistry was evident, and everyone in the room noticed it. After the delivery, Candace and Zion managed to exchange information—and that was the beginning of their love story.

Two years later, Candace and Zion are sitting in their living room holding a beautiful toddler—but not theirs. They are baby-sitting again for Shani.

"You know what?" Zion says. "We're pretty good with this kid. Maybe we should think about getting one for ourselves."

Candace can't stop herself from rolling her eyes. This is a touchy topic that has caused serious conflict a few times. Typically they avoid the subject, but Zion is around mothers and their infants all day; he's been bitten by the baby bug. He wants his own. For her part, Candace is now the executive producer in a male-dominated industry. She wants to enjoy her success and advance awhile longer before settling down. Basically, they are at a stalemate. Every time the issue comes up, Candace feels as though he doesn't understand because he is a man in a successful career and doesn't realize how hard it is for a woman to achieve.

Zion doesn't understand why Candace is all *up in arms* about the issue. She said she wanted to have children, and she's now in her early thirties. He understands there are risks that attend a geriatric pregnancy, which begins after thirty-five. Besides, they are financially stable, and he can comfortably carry things while she can take a couple years off and then rejoin the workforce after their baby becomes a toddler.

In short, they both have emotions that run deep on this issue. Candace's mom stayed home to raise her kids and then never reentered the workforce. And even though they had a happy childhood that was full of love and joy, Candace can't help wondering whether her mom regrets her decision. She has never expressed this to Zion for fear that he wouldn't see her argument as valid. So each discussion about the topic seems to drive a wedge deeper and deeper between them. They seriously need someone to coach them through these murky waters of discontent.

THE POWER OF VULNERABILITY

Many couples have issues that start out small, but because they don't get the proper guidance to navigate through their feelings, the issues unnecessarily become more and more difficult. Talking openly and honestly is not easy if a person thinks their feelings will be invalidated. Nothing is more painful than taking that leap of faith to talk about your emotions and then having them handled carelessly.

That's why vulnerability is an essential ingredient to any successful marriage.

A number of years ago, Wendy and I were coaching a group of young married people in Ohio. I was the new pastor at a church, and as a part of giving to the community, we started a group called Married and Naked. Now, trust me, we've gotten more than enough questions from not too discreet observers who have wondered about the *naked* part of that name.

In truth, the nakedness is purely emotional openness and vulnerability. With many of our couples, the problem wasn't whether they wanted their marriages to work. Neither was it whether they thought they were right all the time or that their spouses were evil. It was simply an issue of knowing how to listen with their hearts and let their spouses express themselves completely without repercussions.

To provide this environment, we developed a technique called *Naked Moments*. And no, this was not a time to shed clothing, but rather a time to shed the tough exteriors we all wear. The intent was to provide couples with a setting where they didn't feel judged or second-guessed. A place where they could express whatever was in their hearts and know the hearer was absolutely willing to listen and then do whatever it took to respond favorably.

Here is how this idea of Naked Moments would work with Candace and Zion.

Candace approaches Zion during a time when there are no conflicts. She simply says, "Zi, I need a naked moment."

The term "naked moment" is a safe word. It is a phrase that indicates something special is about to happen. They are about to enter a deeper level of communication, and there are preparations that need to take place.

When the request is made, it's as though an alarm sounds and the following steps must immediately be activated:

- Zion silences his phone or other electronic devices, such as computers or TVs.
- He goes to Candace and comfortably positions himself to listen by sitting in front of her.

- He is positioning himself to let her know that he is locked in and ready to listen to whatever she has to say.
- There is eye contact and a relaxed posture—another indication that he is interested in whatever her concerns may be.
- He verbally affirms her by letting her know he's ready to listen.
- There is also an unspoken pact of confidentiality. Nothing that is discussed in this moment will ever be brought up as a chance to harm Candace.

This will undoubtedly feel awkward and unnatural when you try this at home. It may even seem as though you're following a script. That's because you are! And you should keep following it until it becomes a natural way of listening. This is necessary within a marriage because we all need to feel secure and safe to express our heart. It's not easy to be completely open without the fear of being hurt, so the listener has to make sure they are completely engaged in hearing and understanding.

Candace then begins. "Honey, I want to talk about why I'm not ready to have a child yet."

If Zion rolls his eyes, takes a deep, frustrated breath, or uses gestures that indicate he doesn't want to hear what she is about to say, he will lose her immediately and the moment will be lost.

By requesting this moment, Candace has opened herself up and has released her defenses so that she can tap into what she is truly feeling.

I often compare this to one spouse giving the other spouse a powerful and potentially dangerous weapon. She has just armed him with firepower and has left herself defenseless. He now has a choice to make. He can take that weapon that she has freely offered and use it to attack her, with all her nerves exposed and her defenses down—a move that will possibly cause irreparable damage to their ability to communicate intimately. Or he can use that weapon to protect her and assure her that he will never let anyone or anything harm her.

This is Zion's chance to show Candace that she can trust him with her heart. This is his opportunity to stand in as her protector. Not because she is weak and can't take care of herself, but because this is what marriage is all about. Each individual should have the freedom to be weak if they choose to be, with the understanding that they won't be taken advantage of.

It makes absolutely no difference who initiates the naked moment. In my experience as a counselor, it seems men have a more difficult time asking for a naked moment because of their perception that it takes away from their masculinity to be emotional. This, of course, is utter nonsense. In truth, men are the ones who could benefit the most from being open and revealing their feelings.

This is the intention behind Naked Moments. The point is to give individuals an opportunity to remove their masks and be in a situation where they can reveal their true hearts and emotions to someone who will listen, understand, and then validate or feel their concerns. The idea is for couples to be able to take off their masks or pretensions and be completely honest with one another.

REMOVING THE MASK

Yes, we all wear masks. Some are unintentional, while others are deliberate. These are the different identities we automatically take on, often without effort, in order to conform to our surroundings. They are emotionally protective coverings.

We wear these chameleonlike guises to hide the things we may be embarrassed about or we don't want to be discovered. They help us, or so we think, to be accepted at our job, school, church, social events, and even in our marriages and close relationships. We wear them to feel protected so that we can cope without our sensitivities being exposed or offended.

These simulated personas we present are often defense mechanisms we may not even recognize because they have been part of us for so long. They are like the guards that stand at the entrance of our heart fortresses, armed with weapons including sarcasm, mean-spirited joking, and avoidance.

My family moved to a new neighborhood in Southern Virginia. I was just entering junior high and was feeling pretty insecure because I was about a hundred pounds dripping wet and came from a very poor family. My dad was disabled and couldn't work, and we lived in a huge, old rented house. My mom practically did everything for the three boys who were left in the home after my sister got married at nineteen and my oldest brother was serving in the Army.

As I did a mental comparison of my life with the lives of who I perceived were the well-to-do kids at my school, I didn't like my conclusions. So I invented a mask. To everyone else, my family had moved to the country from the big city, even though I knew nothing about the city. In fact, I had never really left the town of South Boston, Virginia.

In my made-up world, my dad had a great job and my mom was a housewife and we had a great life when we were in the big city. Since we moved to the country, we'd been simply getting adjusted. That was the story I told the kids at school. I think I may have even spilled that nonsense to a teacher or two. This was who I wanted them to think I was, because I didn't think I'd be accepted for who I actually was. I thought I'd be mortified if they knew I was a poor kid, born and raised in the country, whose family had an outhouse, before moving to this new neighborhood.

I carried this charade on for weeks.

But it wasn't long after socializing and getting to know this new group of students that I came to one startling and sobering realization: I wasn't alone. In fact, most of the people I met were also born in the deep country; some deeper than I. A few of them still had outhouses. Suddenly, my alter ego was not necessary. It became irrelevant when I found that there were others who not only understood but actually lived my life.

This is what adults in relationships must understand. We are all inseparably joined together by similar human experiences and feelings. We are all acquainted with similar insecurities and fears. And sometimes the only way to find this out is if the people closest to us will engage us, listen to us, and create a nonjudgmental, accepting, and attentive environment. That is the essence of Naked Moments.

Marriage is a complex union in which two different individuals are attempting to join every part of who they are, with the sincere hope that each of them will unconditionally accept what is brought to the relationship. The fear of rejection is real, and hiding the person you don't feel your partner will readily accept is common. A great number of relationships that are self-described as "on the rocks" are actually just in need of vulnerability and nakedness.

Honestly consider the following questions: *Does your spouse really know who you are? Are you honestly who you say you are? Are you afraid of being found out, and is the person whom you've hidden terrified of being discovered?*

Being truthful about who you really are is the first step to marital transparency or nakedness. If we do not honestly know who we are, then it will be impossible for our spouse to know or understand the way we think, why we communicate the way we do, how we love, or even our likes and dislikes.

AVOIDING AVOIDANCE

Candace and Zion grew to love each other and became open and honest about who they were to a certain extent. But when it came to those problems they felt might cause conflict, such as having children, they skirted the issue.

I have counseled numerous couples who have gotten in the habit of avoidance. They skirt the real issues and try to just *play nice.* They will do anything and everything not to talk. Like Candace and Zion, it's not that they don't have a good marriage or that they don't love each other. They would just rather deal with some issues on their own as opposed to talking.

Now, that could work if the issue could be handled without affecting the other partner. But the truth of the matter is that very few issues in a successful relationship can be handled without involving your spouse. The person who feels they can just *tough it out* is foolishly deceiving themselves. Besides, what is marriage for if you can't work out problems with the person who is supposed to be the closest to you in the world?

Naked moments are meant to bring out every hidden issue by simply providing the environment to uncover them safely and without judgment. Besides, let's be real! The great majority of times, your spouse has an idea that something is wrong anyway. Your avoiding an issue does not make it nonexistent. It only puts a different face on it and creates a massive issue that everyone knows about, but no one is talking about.

It's like there's a 500-pound gorilla sitting in the middle of the room whenever that hidden topic arises. He doesn't say anything, but just sits there quietly staring at both parties. If either party comes near talking about the subject, you will see the gorilla rise up with excitement and start to wave his hands. But as soon as the issue is avoided or repressed, the gorilla just sits comfortably and stares, waiting to be addressed.

The problem with the gorilla is that if he is not taken out of the room, he will grow. That's because avoidance feeds him. Eventually, there will be less and less space for you to occupy. Your relationship will start to feel closed in and constricted because of this stranger in your home.

Yet here's the strange and powerful fact: You both have control over this beast. For as intimidating as it seems, the issue is directly under your control. Just addressing the gorilla and examining him is the beginning of your healing. Of course, he will fight and scream and sometimes might seem overwhelming, but he can never harm you. He can only posture and scare you.

That is how untreated issues in marriages work. They can be overwhelming when they are not dealt with through emotional nakedness. But the issue is seldom the problem; rather, how you are viewing the issue is the problem. The fact that you see the issue as insurmountable and choose to give up rather than be vulnerable. Or the thought that your spouse will never see it your way or maybe you will never see it her way. These are self-defeating trains of thought destined to keep you enslaved to the problem.

Candace and Zion had one big issue in their marriage. It wasn't unbeatable or too difficult to handle. It only required them mustering up the courage to sit down and spew out everything that was on their mind concerning the issue. The reason they ran into roadblocks was because one of them always felt the other didn't understand and would interrupt. This discouraged the talker and diverted the conversation in another direction. Or someone would roll their eyes, suck their teeth, or make an uncaring gesture that would shut the other person down and start a different argument, usually preceded by the words "You always..." or "You don't ever...!" All the while the gorilla was just chucking down bananas and growing to an unmanageable size. Eventually, he would take over the room and ultimately their marriage.

Let's once again define the steps to defeating this beast:

- Acknowledge its presence. Talk about the thing you don't want to talk about while remembering that you're talking *with* your mate, not *at* them.
- Identify exactly what the gorilla looks like. Be open and honest about the issues. Use a naked moment of uninterrupted speaking to do this.
- Understand that the two of you created the gorilla, or at least allowed it to appear, so both of you must remove it.
- Sometimes the gorilla can be eliminated. Other times, it may be just minimized into an organ-grinder's monkey and tamed. Either way, it must be controlled.

All this can be remedied by disciplining yourself to be emotionally naked in front of your spouse. But the right environment has to be carefully created and managed for this to happen.

Understand that if your mate has the courage to open up and be honestly naked in front of you, then you should have the respect and kindness to honor that openness and allow them to reveal who they truly are and how they feel without any disparagement or criticism. This is how you get to the deeper, more satisfying levels of communication, and that's how you uncover a relationship game changer.

CHAPTER 7

Punks Never Change

Kyle opened his eyes at 6 a.m. from a tough night of trying to sleep. He looked over his left shoulder at a puffy blue night bonnet and sleep mask, under which his wife, Heather, was still lightly snoring. This was a familiar sight. One he had witnessed and pretty much accepted for the last ten years of their marriage. He still loved her and thought she was an awesome wife and mother, but the passionate fire that had excited him when they first met was now just a glowing ember.

Heather woke up moments later and glanced at Kyle, who was shaking off the sleepy cobwebs and starting to get out of bed. He'd slept shirtless throughout their marriage, which was fine when he had a big, broad chest and flat abs. But after years of much food and little exercise, his chest and stomach had switched places. She still loved him but had become disenchanted with their predictable lifestyle. In fact, she had become weary of the direction in which their marriage was going. It seemed that every day repeated itself. Things weren't terrible and they weren't great. They just were.

They had been married for twenty-three years. Both of them were in their late forties and were settled in their careers. Their daughter had just graduated from college and was starting her career, while their errant son was still trying to get out of high school and was *finding his way*.

This was their life. Heather and Kyle. Settled and bored with each other and with everything else.

One day Heather mustered up the nerve to mention her displeasure to her husband.

"Hey, honey, you ever think about when we were first married?"

"Yeah, what in particular?" he asked with curiosity.

"Well, we used to sit down, talk, and laugh for hours. And you used to be so affectionate towards me. We don't ever do that anymore." She was trying to appeal to his kinder side.

"You mean, *I* don't do that anymore, right?" There was obvious offense in his voice. "So you don't like who I am now? The one thing we always said was that we'd let each other be an individual and accept one another for who we are and not try to change each other."

Heather quickly acquiesced, biting her lip and holding her words. She knew he had her dead to rights. After all, that was their marriage narrative and they both knew the script verbatim. It was the main thing they told other young and hopeful couples when asked, "How do you guys do it? How do you stay so happy after all these years?"

We don't try to change each other.

But now those words were coming back to haunt them. Neither

was satisfied with their marriage, but they both felt almost obligated to maintain the façade of acceptance.

AN IMPOSSIBLE STANDARD

Where did we ever get the notion that people are supposed to stay the same from the time they were first married? When you really think about it, the goal seems pretty impossible to accomplish. Furthermore, this is not the same attitude we have in other life relationships.

We don't expect things to stay the same in our career relationships. What if a new banker went to a major financial institution and bucked against a new corporate initiative saying, "You guys hired me like this! You should accept me as I am and *not* expect me to change! In fact, the company should change to accommodate me!" No one in their right mind would dare threaten their job for something so trivial.

What we have to manage in marriage is how to effectively adapt without losing our own identity. Maintaining the core of who you are as you are adapting to your partner can be quite daunting. But those core values, those irreplaceable principles you live your life by, are the very things that made you attractive in the first place. This is the foundation of who you are; the qualities your mate grew in love with.

Just as with individuals, all solid relationships are built on foundations, whether strong or weak. It is easy to determine whether your relationship has staying power by examining the foundation on which it was built. But just as with any building, foundations can shift, become worn or outdated. This happens because, with each passing year, people change and upgrades are required. Our likes and dislikes, habits and attitudes alter because of circumstances and experiences.

I have heard numerous singles looking for love defiantly say that they don't want anyone who will try to change them. "Accept me for who I am" is the mantra that undergirds their singleness. While this may sound liberating, it is not how you grow a relationship. In fact, it's just the opposite. If we are to be honest with ourselves, no one is really willing to accept any person where they meet them without ever changing. The reason is because it is virtually impossible for people not to change!

Before the wedding day is over, you've changed. You've learned what you will never do again or what you will tell your children never to do during their weddings, or what will be a great idea to implement.

This same dynamic plays out in life as well. Each day we are creating new opinions about the things we believe based on the events we experience. The person we will be next month will not be the person we are today, simply because experiences can change us in an instant.

Who you are today may be the result of your best efforts. Congratulate yourself up to this point. However, understand that we are all constantly evolving into the people we want to be. Trial and error, challenges and successes all shape our characters and make us who we are.

For example, a person may love to drive until they are in a terrible car accident. Suddenly they are terrified of getting behind the wheel. Or a child may love a certain food until he eats so much of it that he gets sick. He will begin to dislike that food based on his experience. The food hasn't changed; he has. So our experiences are constantly making us into different people.

Now, I understand the underlying sentiment of not changing. It speaks to not changing the essence of who you are. It means that you won't give up your principles or those things that make you unmistakably you. These are the areas where we feel we will be compromising or sacrificing our soul if we give in.

But honestly, even values can change. Values are your fundamental beliefs that guide how you function or your way of thinking. These may change over time as a person experiences situations that may be life-changing. Someone who is racist will consider that a value until he gets to know a person of a different race and realizes that they share the same struggles and feelings. This realization will change the way he views others and life in general.

So in relationships, change is inevitable. Kyle and Heather were trying to hold on to an

> Here is the straightforward truth: We don't lose ourselves when we change for those we love. This is where we find our true selves. This is where we develop our capacity to love and give.

impossible standard, and it was suffocating their union. They were so busy trying not to change each other that they were not growing together. They were not bending and melding into each other, which is what marriage is all about. This is where the deeper levels of marital love are discovered: in seeing your partner become a part of your world and vice versa. This is where you finish each other's sentences and know one another's intentions without them being mentioned.

Here is the straightforward truth: We don't lose ourselves when we change for those we love. This is where we find our true selves. This is where we develop our capacity to love and give.

Marriage cannot just be launched on the wedding day and then just put on autopilot to a desired destination. Someone actually has to drive the matrimonial vehicle. They have to navigate past obstacles, take detours, and weather tough and unpredictable terrains. They have to stop often to refuel and change the tires when necessary, because on the journey of marriage, things change.

Heather had developed a fear of changing as a child. She saw her mom completely lose herself in her dad and the kids. She felt her mother never really reached her own goals and always accommodated everyone in the family to her own detriment. She determined she never wanted to be that kind of wife and wanted to have complete freedom to be herself. Though she had never spoken to her parents to see whether her assessment of their marriage was accurate, it certainly looked as though her mother served only as a step stool for her dad to reach his heights of success.

This experience planted a seed in Heather's fertile heart, and because it was never confronted, that seed grew into a dysfunctional understanding of change. She wanted to do whatever she could to make her husband happy, but she would always stop short of changing for him. For example, she resisted wearing something he might suggest or changing in any way she felt would detract from who she felt she was.

She refrained from giving Kyle her heart because she didn't want to be hurt like she felt her mom was hurt. She never really trusted Kyle with her total heart because she had seen her mom give and give, with no obvious reward. Her experiences changed her and subsequently left her feeling trapped in a marriage where she wanted change but was afraid to let her guard down.

CHANGE IS INEVITABLE

Change is not only good, it is mandatory. I believe our difficult and positive life experiences happen to us because they are a necessary tool that brings about growth. Every time there is a new experience in our lives, it changes us, whether we want it to or not. And with each alteration, there has to be an adjustment.

I have talked to many couples who have not understood why their marriage was not happy. Why is it that we are stuck in this rut and can't seem to get out? Why have we lost the spark and are now just roommates instead of lovers? What can we do to get things back to the way they used to be?

The answers to all these questions depend on whether the couple has been managing the changes in their marriage. Consider some of the following events and how much of an impact they can have on your relationship:

- Having a baby
- Leaving baby with a sitter
- Buying a new home
- Parent's sickness
- Parent's deaths
- Losing a job
- Financial problems

I'm sure we can add quite a few more events to this list. However, let's look at one of the most life-changing events ever to happen to a couple: childbirth. This is probably the most traumatic, terrifying, exhilarating, confusing, and beautiful occasion in a couple's life. This is one of the pivotal moments that a number of couples dream of.

For as many joys and unimaginable surprises that childbirth can bring, plus the subsequent raising of children, the experience does a serious number on marriages. When a newborn is first introduced into the family, that bouncing, cooing bundle of unconditional love demands the entire room. Everything is focused on the baby. For a while the couple no longer exists. Nothing else has preeminence in the family over the baby and what it wants, when it poops, when it cries, when it eats, whether it sleeps, and if it burps.

However, children in all their splendor can really mess up a marriage if the parents don't understand the impact that child has just had on their lives. As much as I don't want to present children as an interruption, the fact is they are. They interrupt schedules, habits, and freedom; and all these disruptions are wonderfully welcomed by most parents.

But as I've told most parents, you must understand that when that beautiful baby enters your home, it alters things. Most of all, the child affects your relationship. It turns your dyad into a triad. And even though you both may have had nine months to prepare, most couples are seldom ready for how drastic their lives are going to transform.

Often, the parents become so focused on the child that they neglect giving attention to each other. And it's completely understandable. After all, the baby is helpless. Adults can handle themselves, right?

However, it's vitally important to understand that the

mom-and-dad relationship can never replace the husband-and-wife relationship. As unpopular as this statement may be, the marriage relationship is still the most important one in the family dynamic. When the marriage is healthy, the parenting will be so much easier. The child needs to see and feel happy, healthy love between Mom and Dad. But more often than not, couples tend to ignore caring for each other and, with good intentions, focus their affections on the child.

Then you can include the fact that the mother's body has gone through a wringer. Her once smooth and sturdy stomach now resembles a beautifully stretch-marked road map of her pregnancy journey and delivery. There may be C-section scars or other remnants that outline her courageous path. Not to mention emotional changes that may now be a way of life for the new parents.

This is just a snippet of one event that can cause monumental changes in a relationship. I have seen husbands actually feel jealous of the new baby. Even though he may intellectually understand that his feelings are unwarranted, when those emotions are not sufficiently discussed and comprehended, misunderstandings and estrangement can easily be the result.

THE LAW OF MARITAL RECALIBRATION

Change is inevitable in marriage, but how you handle that change is what makes the difference between your success or failure. And with each major event, you must apply what I call the *law of marital recalibration*. This is what you both must do to get your relationship back in sync. You must understand that the equilibrium of the entire relationship rests on how you manage the situations you encounter.

Here's how recalibration works. Understand that married people have a twofold growth dynamic. First, you are growing individually in accordance with your own personal goals and aspirations. You have objectives that you are personally trying to achieve in your career as well as in your own self-development.

This first dynamic of growth is one that you've been developing for most of your life. You had goals as a child to be a doctor, an educator, or an athlete. You may have things you want to accomplish for the benefit of your parents. You want to make sure you are in a place where your mom or dad will be taken care of in their old age. Or maybe you just want to be a positive contributor to the world in some way.

Whatever it is, you have these personal goals that are valuable to you. These are goals that you hold close to your heart. These are your dreams and aspirations. And it is extremely important that you accomplish them and fulfill your desires. Your marriage should not divert you from achieving these aspirations. After all, these wishes existed long before you knew your spouse and should continue to exist to a fuller extent now that you have a partner. At least, that's how it should be. This is the first dynamic of the law.

Here's the second dynamic: You are now married and will grow as a couple. This happens involuntarily. The fact that the two of you have found enough interest in each other to get married should mean that you have found a person with whom you want to grow. So now you are growing as a collective.

This cooperative growth has to do with what you want to accomplish as a family or a partnership. You want to achieve a mutual benefit and reach goals that will leave a legacy for your immediate family's next generations. That may mean the purchase of a home. You may want to start a family. You may want to buy vehicles together. Eventually your kids will go to college or maybe private school.

You have now acquired friends who are a direct result of the two of you being married. There will be traditions and practices that you have as a couple or a family. There are many other couple practices that you participate in. These are your marriage goals.

Next, we look at where these two dynamics will either find nexus or conflict. Remember, these two trajectories, personal and marital goals, are advancing sometimes together and sometimes at different paces. This is the challenge when it comes to change in relationships. How do you manage both routes? Because they will continue moving whether you want them to or not. The question is, which path will you prioritize?

In order for a marriage to work effectively, these two dynamics must coexist and feed on each other. If the marriage dynamic is thriving but the personal one is subdued, a spouse may feel as though they are losing themselves in the marriage or in the other spouse. This is when a wife may feel as though she has sacrificed her personal goals and success for her marriage. She may have had to leave work to raise the kids or even not gone back to school because family and life got in the way. Everything is now about marriage and family, and she doesn't know who she is anymore.

Likewise, the husband may feel his life has reached a roadblock because he had to make personal sacrifices just to maintain family stability. He may have had to stay at the same job and couldn't even think of taking the risk of looking into a different career path. His goals of personal achievement are on the back burner, along with his excitement about his marriage.

If the individual component is growing and being fed but the marriage dynamic is neglected, the other spouse may feel abandoned. This is where Heather and Kyle found themselves. They were so intent on fiercely maintaining individuality and not changing each other that their marriage was beginning to stagnate. They were both growing and pursuing their personal successes to the detriment of their relationship, and the kids were caught in the middle. It was only a matter of time that they would begin to see the marriage as not as important as their personal achievements.

Achieving personal goals is not the same as achieving marital goals. Some couples may feel that if they can just be the best they can be separately, it will benefit the marriage. This never happens.

Marriage is an entity all by itself. Though it comprises two distinct individuals, it is a whole new entity. Think of your marriage as a living and breathing creature that the two of you created. You gave it life. It is an institution that will grow, breathe, and prosper commensurate with the effort and attention you give it. It cannot exist without mutual attention. It cannot thrive with just one person feeding it. It must be nurtured by both parties.

When two people create a marriage, it becomes dependent on each individual in order to exist. You cannot just keep doing what you did when single and expect this new creation to thrive. Even though you should never lose your own desire for personal achievement, now that you've created the marriage, the personal and the marriage goals must harmonize.

Both parties must be committed to managing both dynamics either simultaneously or in stages. This can be done in different ways. I have seen couples decide they are going to both pursue their own personal goals and find a sitter or nanny to help with the children. They will come together daily to focus on their marriage and family, but neither will abdicate their personal pursuits. And as long as everyone has mutually agreed upon the plan of action, this can work well.

Other couples will choose to have one spouse focus on the family and children while the other focuses on the income and providing for the family. This may go on until the kids are older and the spouse at home can then pursue his or her goals. This can also work well; as long as it is fully understood that there will be equality in value even though there may be a difference in function. Both must see each role as equally valuable and honorable.

A great number of couples may not even consider that there is an actual necessity to calibrate their marriages on a consistent basis because of the constant change. That they need to actually decide how they are going to manage the working dynamics in their relationship. They merely amble along in their marriages, not noticing that each event in their lives is shifting the foundation of their marriage.

COMMUNICATE TO RECALIBRATE

So here's how recalibration works: The key to managing this constant change is continual communication. It's vital that couples notify each other when they feel something has had an impact on them. After every signal event in a family's life, there should be a discussion to recalibrate and discover how each person in the family has been changed.

With each major situation, there must be a coming together to discuss who you are now, after the situation has occurred. Sometimes there may have to be a professional counselor in the room to facilitate, but communicating about the occurrence is essential so that both of you can understand where you are and then adjust accordingly.

This may seem tedious to some. Shouldn't people just roll with the punches and get over it? I wish it were that easy. Often, we never really know just how any of us will be affected by a significant life event or situation. Most of us think we can handle just about anything, until it happens.

But the truth is that it takes time and intentional focus to manage married life together. This is why it's so important to communicate what you're going through after major happenings in your family. Notify each other when you have changed. This means taking time out of your pursuits to sit down and talk about issues.

Let's be honest. No one likes to talk about this stuff! No one looks forward to it at the end of the day, but *wanting* to talk about something is inconsequential. You talk because you want to preserve and grow the relationship. And because we are always growing either individually or collectively, if you are bent on not changing or feel that you don't have to tell your spouse when you've been affected, you *will* ultimately grow apart.

This is a painful place to be in a relationship, where both parties have just accepted the fact that they are not connecting and they let things fall apart. When this happens, resentment and emotional separation are sure to follow. Each spouse will start to see the other and the marriage as having less value. It is a sure way to lose everything.

It is understood that we all have massive imperfections as partners. None of us has escaped challenges. And all of us conceal our issues under fear. While it may be scary to take off the façade that protects us, this is vital in the healing process. Identify the changes that have taken place in your life, take an honest assessment of them, and reveal them to your spouse. When you truly understand what is behind the way your spouse acts, it becomes easy to accommodate the changes or at least have a clear picture of what you're dealing with.

Many couples have gotten into ruts where they want better for their relationship, but just don't know how to get there. They remember how it used to be and want those feelings again. The challenge has not been that they dislike each other or have not loved each other. They have just become so accustomed to routine that the marriage flame that had excited them from early in their marriage is now flickering.

Kyle and Heather had pledged their love and undying affection to each other with families and friends present in a beautiful ceremony. What had stood as the cornerstone for their relationship was that they would accept each other for who they were. They never wanted to try and *change* each other. While this may sound all well and good, it is an unrealistic assertion that does not make for an exciting marriage.

They needed to understand that before they were married, they were two individuals with two different objectives in life. They were going in different directions. He had his journey and she had hers. They had to answer to no one and were accountable only to their own ambitions. This is how single people are supposed to live, and it's a good thing.

But that journey can get lonely, especially after you have acquired some reasonable success in your quest. You have the career you desire, the home you want, and the friendship circle you love. All is well, until you go home for the night alone. You pull into your empty garage and walk into your quiet home, with maybe your excited and anxious French bulldog, Roxie, begging to go out for a walk.

After your evening routine of takeout and TV, you turn in for the night and realize there is no warm body next to you. Roxie just won't do the job of providing human comfort and companionship. So you want to *change* your situation. You want someone to *share* your life with. You want a *partner* whom you can love. Change, share, partner—all words that have a lot to do with altering your direction.

I've heard many singles utter these words, so it amazes me that once they are in a relationship, they forget that the main reason they wanted one was to change what they had before. They wanted something different. Someone with whom they could share the good times and the bad.

Now they're married and have the potential to have just that. They have the grand opportunity to personally and intimately witness someone else's life. They have the honor to be allowed into another person's mind and experience their pain and their pleasure. So now they must consider whether it is feasible to keep going in their different individual directions or find a new direction where they both have to bend in order to arrive at a mutually agreed upon destination.

If there is going to be any happiness or joy in a relationship, it must be open to becoming different than it was when it began. It just wasn't reasonable for Heather and Kyle to hold on with a death grip to their individuality if they wanted to stay married. There is a great beauty in altering some of who you are to please the person you love. And there is an equal beauty in knowing that your mate loves you so much that they, too, are willing to correct or eliminate those things that are not corresponding to your mutual happiness.

This is what marriage is all about. This is why we become legally bound to another person. So that we can influence each other and together become more powerful than we could have ever been alone.

CHAPTER 8

Punks Resist Boundaries

Tyson was shopping one day at the local department store in suburban Dublin, Ohio. He was just about to check out when he heard a few girls in front of him laughing as they looked at the tabloids on the rack. All were local girls who had grown up in that mostly Caucasian area. Tyson saw that one of them, Jessica, had dropped her wallet right at his feet. Without thinking, he gently tapped her on the shoulder to alert her that her wallet had fallen as he bent over to pick it up, but the other girls noticed at the same time.

Jessica was more taken by Tyson's handsome dark features than she was shocked at her fallen wallet. Her friends were not so much impressed. Their curious and slightly condescending glances told him the entire story. He saw looks that were all too familiar to a young black man in a mostly white environment. Yet Jessica went out of her way to say thank you and, moments later, waited outside the store, to the dismay of her friends, to offer him her number.

Tyson and Jessica went out on their first date. Neither of them had dated interracially, although Tyson was open to it. They were surprised by how easy they got along. They both felt awkward when they went out, since occasionally they would get a curious disapproving glance, but they felt their love would conquer all. They agreed to avoid any racially sensitive conversation and not see color in their relationship.

Unfortunately, that didn't work for either of their parents, who both saw color clearly. Tyson and Jessica were met with opposition from both sides. Tyson's parents felt that Jess could not relate to the black struggle, and that he was not giving girls of his race a chance. Jess's parents felt Tyson was nice, but white should marry white. That's just how it's supposed to be.

Against their parents' wishes, they decided to marry—maybe out of defiance, or maybe as an attempt to show how strong their love actually was. Regardless, they married and shortly after had a baby.

After nearly a year, they were forced to confront the race issue when Tyson felt discriminated against at work. He came home angry and wanted to share his frustration with Jess. She tried to get him to see the other side, but he thought she was trying to ignore obvious discrimination. The argument intensified. Out of frustration, Tyson stood up and called Jessica privileged and out of touch. He said she could never understand him or what he went through on a daily basis.

This touched a nerve in her, so she stood up as well, surprised and hurt that he would even think that. Without a second thought, she said, "Tyson, I can't believe you would say that. Why are you acting like a [*N-word*]?"

The room went silent. Only the gentle cooing of their baby could be heard. Jessica was shocked that the word had come out of her mouth, and she knew Tyson would not give her a chance to explain. He stood there stunned as all the warnings he had heard from his friends and family came back to haunt him. Without another word, he grabbed his jacket and walked out.

Jessica broke down into tears. Not knowing what to do, she picked up her phone and called me, incoherently muttering what had happened between her sobs. We now needed to see if we could salvage their severely damaged marriage.

A SPECIAL CHALLENGE

When two people of different races marry, there will be inherent disparities. As much as I wish it wasn't so, it is. There are behaviors that may be completely different because of how each person views society and how a particular culture or race has been viewed or treated. These cannot be denied. Neither can we have the naïve hope that it won't matter because we love each other.

Cultural differences exist in interracial marriages, but believe it or not, those differences are not the reason there is conflict. Racial differences were not the reason Tyson and Jessica were having marriage trouble. Neither were their families' objections the cause of their difficulty. In fact, many couples have married interracially or interculturally and have loved and learned from each other until a ripe old age.

The truth is that there are different levels of challenges in all relationships. Spouses may have different upbringings or have varying family dynamics. They may be from dissimilar social classes or experiences. There may be religious or spiritual differences. The list can go on indefinitely. For as different as people are, their struggles can be different.

It is ridiculous or at the very least shortsighted to expect that your marriage will not experience consequences from any of these deep-seated issues. There are numerous layers of difficulty in every relationship. Therefore, you must be intentional about making sure you are not fighting against each other as you peel through those layers. Challenges are normal in a marriage, and racial differences are just one of many possible issues.

The most successful interracial or intercultural couples are those who have accepted the fact that there are differences, be they race, culture, class, age, economics, etc. They actually see color, which is absolutely fine. The most reasonable thing is to see the differences in each other and accept them.

We all have a deep desire to be compatible in our relationships. There are some areas in which a couple will be completely compatible. They may like the same genre of movies or the same pastimes. They may have the same sense of humor or the same odd way of looking at life. These are the common compatibilities we look for in another person.

Then there are compatible differences. These are where a couple will have different qualities, but they will fit together perfectly. She likes to be in public and he likes to be behind the scenes. He loves to cook and she loves to clean. He sees the big picture and she is an incredible planner and implementer. This is the essence of the puzzle fit. They are complete opposites, but those opposing qualities are completely necessary to make the whole picture fit together.

The trouble comes when spouses choose to ignore the obvious

fact that each partner has had different life experiences. You cannot completely disregard what society sees as an obvious difference, especially since you have to live in that society. You cannot simply act as though the disparities are not present. What a couple can do is embrace those differences and then establish boundaries so that the two of you will understand what is and what is not allowed.

In my experience, there seems to be this blind belief that once you are married, everything should just automatically fall in place. This couldn't be further from the truth. Where complex differences exist in a relationship, a couple must have stop gaps in place to know when they have crossed the line and these boundaries must be strictly and sternly adhered to.

THE BLESSING OF BOUNDARIES

Let's define what boundaries in marriage are. These are limitations that the two of you have shared based on your personal pain or life experiences. These are the sensitive areas in your life where no one is privy to tread—not even your spouse.

A wife may have come from an abusive home, where voices were raised constantly. Her husband needs to understand that during an argument, loud arguing may be a boundary or trigger that causes her to close down. These areas of sensitivity must be discovered and respected if progress is to be made in the relationship.

This may seem to go against conventional wisdom about marriage. Some have believed that when you are married, you can completely be yourself. That is the goal—eventually. But it takes time to get to that point of marital bliss where you don't have to watch your words or you are free to discuss anything without

> **No one ever said marriage was supposed to be easy. It's supposed to be beneficial!**

limitations; where you don't have to be concerned about your spouse being offended or offending you. This is only achieved through a great deal of time, failure, recovery, and trust. It's not an easy thing, but no one ever said marriage was supposed to be easy. It's supposed to be beneficial!

Back to boundaries. Think of it this way. When you buy a home, there is a surveyor who defines the borders of your property. Those boundaries tell you where your property begins and ends. No one has a right to come onto your property without permission or unless they are really comfortable with you and there is a mutual understanding.

When Wendy and I were first married, we rented a home with a big backyard. It was in a neighborhood adjacent to other homes with large backyards. However, our yard had a beautiful custom-made playhouse and swing, and the other homes had kids. We had just moved in, so we had no relationship with the neighbors or their children. The owners who were there before us did have a relationship with the neighbors.

Well, imagine our dismay when early one morning we heard the sounds of children yelling and playing in our playhouse and swinging on our swing. These kids were on our property! They had crossed our boundaries and taken liberties based on their previous relationship. Wendy and I felt a little encroached upon. The neighbors did not have the same privileges with us that they had with the previous occupants.

Hence, this is how relationship boundaries work. There are areas in our lives where it's perfectly okay to let some people enter because we have a relationship and we feel comfortable with them. However, when you enter into a new relationship, you can't use those same old boundaries. You cannot live by the rules from your previous situation, and it's not reasonable or fair to expect your current relationship to abide by the rules of your past.

It takes several elements for a relationship to get to a place where boundaries can be relaxed and crossed without harm. These are communication, time, and proven trust.

Tyson and Jessica had never communicated about the obvious differences in their marriage. They had spent no time on that particular issue, so trust never entered the picture. They merely assumed they both knew how to handle their differences, and they were terribly wrong.

For them to seek healing, they had to go back and talk about the obvious and discover the reasons they really got married. She honestly revealed that she was rebelling against her parents, whom she felt were racist, but she really missed her friend group, who had ignored her since she married Tyson. He admitted that he really didn't trust her race and his family didn't either, and what she called him proved that he was correct. They had to discover what their boundaries were and how they could rebuild their marriage with those boundaries in place, until they could get to a point to trust completely.

Unfortunately, the hurt was too deep. Tyson and Jessica mutually chose to end the marriage, but the lessons learned were invaluable. They understood that marriage does not give you a license to speak your mind without restraint. It doesn't give you the freedom to spew whatever is in your heart.

Speaking of speech, one key to successful relationships is to know when to speak and what to say. There are some things you simply will not be able to do until your spouse feels safe around you. There is some behavior you may have to renounce because it seriously touches on some unhealed hurt in your partner's life.

For example, let's say a person has been in a verbally abusive relationship. There was screaming and very aggressive verbal confrontations that came just short of physical violence. There were nasty insults to the point where the relationship had to be ended. Now that same person is in a new relationship with a kind and gentle person.

But one day, he raises his voice in jest to his spouse, and she cringes and reacts as though he has seriously offended her. He's confused. She's offended. They're now in a full-blown conflict because he's wondering why she would get so upset over something so trivial. She, on the other hand, was just sent back to her previous abuse.

Raising his voice was a boundary for her. It must be communicated that an angered tone is a boundary. The more she sees that he is aware of it, the more she will begin to trust.

NOT ALL BOUNDARIES ARE CREATED EQUAL

Jessica and Tyson were not ready for the difficult relationship they chose to be in. They did not consider the fact that each of them had personal beliefs and boundaries that were vitally important to them. They chose not to reveal what those limits were basically because they did not know it was necessary. They believed that love was enough to conquer all.

Is it any wonder that most bright-eyed lovers can only see the euphoria? The realities come only after the glee has worn off. And one of the most difficult truths to grasp about boundaries is that not all boundaries are created equal.

It would seem that this is contrary to the entire concept of boundaries. Many marriage turf wars have been fought because one person is retaliating after not getting a quid pro quo or a fair shake when it comes to boundaries.

Let's go back and recap Jessica and Tyson's fateful argument. It was a normal day. Tyson came home from work and Jessica was there with the baby. But today, he was very frustrated about feeling slighted by his superior on his job. He was upset and needed to vent.

Jessica was willing to listen and did just that. She offered her opinion about how he was reacting, which she had every right to do. She told him things were probably not as bad as he was thinking and maybe he was exaggerating the conflict.

As a person of color, he felt that his gripes were valid and that he had every right to voice his complaints to his wife. He felt that he had been passed over because of his race. When she retorted, he was upset and told her so: She was privileged and could not understand his plight.

Now, from a wife's perspective, this was a painful statement. The woman you married and pledged your life to, who has been with you through many struggles, doesn't understand you? That could be taken as a legitimate insult. Jessica's response rose out of that pain because she wanted him to know how she felt. He had insulted her. She not only needed to let him know that, but also needed him to know that he was not acting like the man she married. He was acting like an N-word.

Of course, her response was just as insulting as his—in her

mind. But there was a vast difference from his perspective. Truly both were in complete fight mode and they were trading insults. One insult should not be any worse than another. Right? Besides, Jessica didn't tell Tyson that he *was* the N-word; she simply said he was *acting* like one. So why all the drama and the deep hurt?

They had both crossed boundaries. They had both disrespected each other. They had both been definitely out of line, but not all boundaries are created equal.

When we are looking at boundaries, the one thing that must be understood is that each person's boundaries are constructed based on their personal life experiences. There is no universal blueprint on how to draw them. There is no collective understanding of which are reasonable and which are not. Boundaries are highly subjective based on the experiences of the person who is drawing them.

My wife and I have had this argument on many occasions to the point where we now have become completely comfortable with it; it's humorous even. If I do something that she dislikes, she will check me and let me know that was not something she appreciates. When she says that, my involuntary response is, "But you did the same thing to me!"

This is where we laugh about it. She will ask, "When I did it, did it bother you?"

I know where she's going with this line of questioning, so I will begrudgingly respond, "No, it did not."

To which she will reply, "Okay, then these boundaries are not created equal. You're not bothered, but I am."

Now, 99 percent of the people reading this will say, "That's not fair!"

On the contrary. Let's take a closer look at this. Couples often have things they don't agree on. They have varying tastes and different styles. They may even have different friends and different things they find enjoyable. This is what being an individual is all about. You do not lose who you are just because you are legally and morally binding yourself to another person. In fact, if it's done correctly, you should enhance your individuality because of the union.

This diversity is also true when it comes to boundaries in your relationship. For as different as you are, you have different areas that may be sensitive. Depending on your life experiences and events that have happened, you will vary in what offends you.

But this is where the difficulty comes in. One spouse will be offended by the very thing they themselves may do. They may hate to have anyone raise their voice at them, when they do the exact same thing to their spouse.

Is this unfair? Of course it is. But is it hypocritical? Absolutely not, because the other spouse is not offended. When it comes to boundaries, you cannot look at them from the perspective of what's fair or impartial.

Before you pull your hair out in disbelief that I would dare to say it's okay not to be impartial in marriage, let's be brutally honest for a moment. Do you expect your spouse to contribute the exact and precise qualities to your marriage that you do? Do you expect completely equal input when it comes to finances, chores, child rearing, or even sexual desire? I would venture to say no! You don't. And if you do, please read the rest of this book, because your marriage is in trouble.

When you really think about it, relationships are rampant with double standards and unfairness. Individuals bring different amounts of money to a marriage. They have different talents or areas of expertise. They have differing goals and ideologies on social issues and life in general.

In summary, there is no such thing as a completely equal or fifty-fifty marriage. There are few things humans do that are completely equal. Neither are boundaries equal. They shouldn't be because you are different people. So don't expect equality when it comes to boundaries and sensitive areas.

If your wife is offended when you are late, yet she's late consistently, she's not being a hypocrite. She's being human. People are not machines, and we often expect to receive things we may not give.

When discussing boundaries with your spouse, it's important that you focus only on what seriously offends them. And if you do not share the same emotional limitation, do not create a false boundary in retaliation, just to be equivalent with the one they have in an attempt to *be fair*. The objective is for you to focus only on the things that honestly offend you. Concocting tit-for-tat boundaries will make communication even more difficult.

It takes a great deal of personal discipline not to retaliate when your partner seems to do the very thing they require that you don't do. But this is where real marriage begins to show itself. This is where authentic love exists.

I see this personally when I witness my wife avoiding certain topics with me, even though I have approached the same subjects with her. However, she understands that I may have a sensitivity in that area that she does not, and vice versa. Now, I know a lot of people reading this will say, "But if you don't want it done to you, don't do it to others." That may sound fair and correct, but people are flawed and it takes time and patience to fight the urge to retaliate and instead respect each other's subjective boundaries.

It does not always work as smoothly as I'm portraying it. Even between Wendy and me, there has been and probably will still be some discord along the way, when new boundaries are discovered as life advances. That's right. As life goes on, and relationships grow, new boundaries may be discovered and established.

For example, let's say that Tyson and Jessica found the strength and forgiveness to make their marriage work. They talked about their history and sensitivities and decided to stay. Without question, they would have had to establish new boundaries.

It has to be understood here that marriages are dynamic, not static. They are ever growing, ever changing and renewing; just as the individuals are constantly changing. With all change and new experiences, there should be a readjustment and a revamped understanding of how each person has been affected by those changes and whether there are any recent boundaries to consider.

I have seen this happen in quite a few relationships. They will go through numerous life-altering experiences but will continue to function like they did from the beginning. In every profession and pursuit in life, there is a readjustment to the newest thing happening. Employees are mandated to go through continuing education to bring themselves up-to-date on the latest trends and policies.

I clearly remember my first computer, which weighed about a ton and made that electronic waking up, static noise when you went on the internet. You also had to access the web by using a disk operating system, or DOS. It was cutting edge. That is, until Microsoft changed the game completely and you had to adjust, then came all the other platforms to make computer life easier. You had to readjust to the trends.

I'm amazed by the ease with which we are willing to adjust to technology or social trends and follow new rules. Yet some consider it too much work to follow new rules in relationships and set new boundaries. People change more than technology. We change by the minute and therefore more communication and adjustments are required as we evolve.

If you plan to stay married and have a great happiness track record, you must completely do away with the unrealistic notion that things have to be equal. His desires do not have to match hers. Her boundaries may not be his boundaries, so don't pretend one exists just to make things appear fair. When you truly care about someone and want them to feel protected, you're perfectly fine with tending to their challenges even if you can't relate to what they're feeling.

This is what loving and respecting someone looks like. When you commit to love, it may not always seem fair. You may have to put your feelings aside and just focus on the challenges your spouse is dealing with. Your time will come later. Sacrifice until that time and understand that boundaries don't have to be fair, but they have to be respected.

CHAPTER 9

Punks Fall in Love

Josh and Debbie are fed up with each other and with their marriage. They both feel it's just too draining! They married later in life after having spent most of their lives building their careers.

Josh was forty-five when he first met Debbie at a friend's birthday party. He saw her before she noticed him, and he had every intention of getting her alone to talk to her. He had spent the last twenty years building his franchise. Now as the proud owner of his own company, he was ready to settle down. Although he had no problem meeting women, no relationship seemed to have any staying power. They were all too needy for his taste or too independent; too bossy or too docile; too frumpy to date or too sexy to be a wife. Needless to say, Josh had very discriminating tastes in women.

But regardless of his prolific dating experiences, he felt it was time to settle down and find a wife. He wasn't sure if he wanted children, so hopefully his potential wife would already have kids.

Since he had built quite a comfortable life for himself, the only thing he needed was someone to complete the puzzle.

Debbie had spent a great deal of time building a life for herself and her teenage son as well. She had dropped out of college after getting pregnant by her boyfriend, who abandoned her. As a single mom, she struggled to go back to school years later and get her degree. She had recently finished an intensive program to become a nurse practitioner. Because she had spent so much time focusing on providing for her son, who was now in college, she had put dating in the back of her mind. At forty-one, she considered it likely that she would never find her soul mate. That is, until she was invited to her sorority sister's birthday party.

Josh was the man she dreamed about. He was debonair, articulate, and well established. He was fine with not having a biological child. After the party, they sat in his car all night and just talked. There was no physical intimacy, just in-depth and revealing conversation. They were amazed by the things they had in common, and they laughed so hard, it was ridiculous! A follow-up date was simply understood.

They both realized that since they were older, a lot of the dating protocol could be circumvented. So after only six months of dating, they eloped to a tropical island and got married. It was a whirlwind adventure filled with romance, excitement, and fantasy. It was everything they could have hoped for.

Fast-forward two years later. According to Debbie, she has tried *everything* to feel what they felt when they were first married; nothing works. She doesn't want to feel empty inside anymore. They don't enjoy being around each other. In fact, they have much more fun around their friends than each other. Debbie's crestfallen face and slumped posture tell the story more accurately than her words ever could.

She insists, "I don't feel like I love him or he loves me anymore."

Josh feels that his eyes are beginning to wander. He fantasizes about other women. Debbie has just lost it for him. She's still a nice person and he wants what's best for her, but he doesn't have any sexual desire for her. It doesn't feel like it used to when they met. He just doesn't know how to get beyond this point, and he's not sure he wants to.

According to him, "I love her, but I'm just not *in love* with her anymore."

FORGET FALLING

I wish I could find the person who concocted that phrase. He or she obviously had never been in a long-lasting marriage. The L-word, when spoken about a romantic relationship, strikes fear into most hearts for a number of reasons. The idea of *falling into* this mysterious quagmire of emotional commitment is comparable to enlisting in the military. It has decent financial benefits, three meals a day, a comfortable place to sleep, and great companionship. However, there is this constant looming fear that at any given moment a deadly war could erupt and you could wind up fighting for your life. For this reason, many either shy away or deny they are ever in it.

There is a reason people have this opinion of love and why they equate it with falling into something. That's because many feel there is a helplessness to being in love. *I'll find it one day*, or, *When it happens, you'll know*. It's as though love is a mysterious, amorphous essence floating around in the air, or maybe it's more like a viral infection that's caught by those who are unguarded until it's too late.

This notion of love being unpredictable adds to its mystery and romanticizes the idea of how special it is to many. Then add to this the overwhelming feelings that a person experiences when they "fall in love." The uncontrollable urge to be around this adorable soul and share all your life with him. You wake up and she is the first thought on your mind and the last vision before you close your eyes to sleep. Spending time together makes you forget about food and you don't want to listen to anyone's negative counsel or opinions about him.

And the physical reactions that arise because of these feelings even intensify the idea of love. Every time he sees her, his manhood awakens and beckons to manifest itself, so he has to intentionally keep it in check. Her body heat increases significantly, and her womanhood is summoning and begging him to quench her thirst.

Honestly, if you look at love from this perspective, it's easy to see why many associate it with feelings. I mean, seriously, this stuff feels awesome! Who wouldn't want to be overcome by this? Who wouldn't want this to look forward to—to have someone who feels this way about you?

And then, these feelings can grow even deeper. The good feelings may start off at a minimal level, but then they grow into something enormous and simply out of control. Let's face it: Love feels amazing!

But let's take a closer look at this notion of *falling in love*. It has become such a commonplace understanding that it's taken for granted that this is how love happens. You fall into it. And once you're there, you're *in love*. No one knows how it truly happens or whether you can predict it or prevent it. It just happens; hence the idea of *falling*. But what actually happens when something or someone falls into anything? I've had my share of falling experiences throughout my life, so I'll use my own examples.

I fell down once in middle school and broke my collarbone. I didn't mean to do it! My friends and I were playing around as though we were all Bruce Lee when I quickly realized I wasn't. It was an accident, though. I wasn't looking for the fall; it just happened. My feet went up in the air and I came down on my shoulder and that was that. I had nothing to do with the actual break, but I did participate in the roughhousing, so I guess I had to take it like a man, or at least a twelve-year-old. I'm still not sure if the fall or the uncontrollable crying was more humiliating.

A bird's poop once fell on my head. I guess I was in the right place at the wrong time. The excrement was falling at a speed that was proportionate to the speed of my walking pace, so that at the exact time our paths juxtaposed, the unfortunate occurrence happened and I had bird crap in my hair. The bird meant no harm by it, and I sure didn't invite it. It just happened. I was embarrassed and it was messy, but I survived.

I'm sure you get the picture by now. *Falling in love* is a great romantic notion, but it has its pitfalls. It indicates a lack of control and randomness. It depicts love as floating out there like a disease or like a puddle that someone steps into accidentally after it rains.

Falling is always painful and is often accompanied by injury. There is no rhyme or reason to it. It may or may not happen. And the idea that this is the same random and indiscriminate way we find love, form lifelong bonds, have children, buy houses, and build communities is pretty disturbing.

Let me share three observations of how the idea of *falling in love* influences us in negative ways.

No Responsibility

First, the idea of *falling in love* takes the responsibility of love out of the hands of the lover and gives it to some haphazard occurrence that bases its success on timing and being in the correct place.

It's so much easier to depend on love as a random act than to actually feel accountable as to when or if it happens. The idea that a person was *lucky* to find love gives the credit to love and not to the person who is actually involved in it. It pictures love as a thing that lurks around hiding and waiting to pounce on the unsuspecting searcher. So if you're in the right place at the right time, you'll be blessed by it.

We have all seen modern representations of the Roman god Cupid. This infantile, naked, milky white, cherubic, humanlike person flies about observing people interacting romantically. And if you're not careful, he will take out his arrow and pierce your heart, and without any help from you, now you're in love.

This myth has pervaded our general understanding of love for eons. Whether we believe in Cupid or not, the idea still persists and has burned into our minds the irresponsible randomness of how love begins. No wonder people don't feel responsible for whom they love or if they love. They didn't do it, Cupid did! And if the arrow falls out, they are not *in love* anymore. They can just walk away.

But here's the ironic part: We often attribute the possession of love to chance. Yet when it comes to the maintenance of love, I have not talked to anyone who has sued Cupid for breach of warranty. No one blames the pixie. There are no accusations of assault and battery because he shot us with his arrow. I believe that is because deep down we all have a feeling that the notion is ludicrous. We just don't know how to make it tangible or real.

No Hope

Second, the notion of *falling in love* leaves many people feeling hopeless and doubtful because they have to depend on an unknown variable for their happiness.

We all want to be happy and experience love. But the idea that something so vital to our long-lasting happiness is so imprecise and unpredictable breeds hopelessness. The fact that we can take control of our careers, our finances, and our homes but have no control over love is disheartening to say the least. It leaves us still feeling a degree of failure in our lives, because we have not been able to obtain this elusive prize, even with all the other successes we may have attained.

I can't begin to count how many hopeful people who desire love feel so defeated because it hasn't found them. They are still waiting for it to happen. And since it's something you fall into, they are patiently waiting to catch the virus or step into the abyss. *When will I find love? Does Cupid know I exist? Does he have my address?*

There is nothing more defeating than this notion. I know because I have heard the despair in the voices of many single people who have not found love. I have also listened to the pain of many married couples who feel they are in relationships where love has never existed. Or what they *thought* was love wasn't really that at all. This sadness is real and it can be devastating when someone believes they have to wait for something and have no idea as to whether it will ever arrive.

No Input

Third, because the lover is not responsible for love, they now have no input as to whether it stays or leaves, which causes instability and insecurity.

So now that you have been lucky enough to *find* love, the big question is how long will it stay? You, of course, have no control over that because you fell into it. You didn't see it and you weren't aware of its existence. Before you knew it, it was all over you and now you have no control over how long it will stick around. This leaves the lovers always fearful and wondering whether today will be the day that it leaves.

"Do you still love me?" is the fearful question many people in relationships ask when there is a marital challenge. It's as though people are waiting to see if it will evaporate or if Cupid will repossess his arrow.

I believe that people spend entire lives without ever experiencing love because they are so intent on falling into it. But the fact is, love has never been this arbitrary. It is not about what you feel for the person in your relationship.

Many make the mistake of thinking that the greater the feeling, the greater the love. So when the feelings are gone, so is the love. This may sound like a normal way of experiencing this elusive feeling, but it is a punkish way of looking at love. When people measure love by how they feel about another person, they are constantly *falling* in and out of it countless times throughout their lives. Who wants to live like that?

Here is an unapologetic truth: You have just as much input into whether or not you experience love as you do in whether or not love leaves. The idea that it can wake up one morning, pack its bags, call Cupid to say it's quitting, and hit the road is not close to being correct. No one has to lose love, even if they lose the object to which it is directed.

LOVE IS A DECISION

Josh and Debbie married because they were *in love*. They were expecting to be old and gray, lying in each other's arms breathing their last breath together. They had every hope that love would keep them together and accomplish this.

We call on love to be at the foundation of building our families, buying a house, and doing the things that married people do. Yet we have come to believe that love is a capricious feeling that has no real basis, except in increased heartbeats and a swelling in our loins. There has to be more.

My purpose for writing this chapter is to demystify love and take it out of fairyland and bring it into the real world, where actual people live, cry, laugh, smile, get angry, insult, forgive, recover, and then do it all over again.

So what is love and how do we get it?

Love begins with a desire to be committed, and then it follows through with a decision to commit. This means that one must want to be in love before actually experiencing it. Then he or she must be willing to make the decision to follow through. That's right! A decision. Love begins with a decision, and that is why so many don't ever experience it. They are terrified of making the decision to love.

Let me talk a little about my own love story. It was a sunny afternoon and I was leaving a somewhat lackluster church service when I walked out of the building and saw this woman standing just a few feet away from me. She was tall and lean with a long ponytail that hung down below her shoulders. I positioned to try and see her face but was hindered by a pair of huge fashionable sunglasses, which covered what seemed like three quarters of her face.

As I stood there for a moment mysteriously fixed on this stranger, someone grabbed my arm. It was my friend Sarah.

"Calvin, come with me," she shamelessly said with no explanation. Sarah had never done this before, so I was surprised and intrigued.

She took me to a place on the large front stoop of the church where fewer people were gathered and said, "Stand here. I'll be right back."

To my amazement, she had done the same thing to this stranger I had noticed when I first left the building, and there she was standing in front of me.

Sarah said, "You two need to meet," and then just as abruptly as she had performed this forced introduction, she disappeared.

Wendy, who I found out was a church greeter, reached out her hand and said, "Hello, and welcome. I hope you had a great time at church."

I was torn between lying about having a great time and offending her with the fact that I was bored out of my mind. So I chose to lie. "It was great! I'm Calvin."

She asked, "Are you new here?"

"No, I live in DC and just chose to come to church with my sons today," I responded to what seemed to be a canned greeting.

"Oh!" she replied. "Where are your sons?"

I proudly pointed to the two handsome young men on the stoop below. "Over there, waiting for me, I'm sure."

"Wow!" she replied, finally breaking protocol from her practiced speech. "They're handsome!"

I saw this as an opening to know her better, so I interjected, "Yes, I agree, but what about their dad?"

I saw that she was obviously thrown off her greeting game but smiled and immediately there was a connection. We ended the conversation pleasantly and I left the venue.

Was it love at first sight? Not hardly. If I had never seen her again, I may have regretted missing an opportunity, but life would have progressed just splendidly. She may have remembered the brief connection, but then the memory would have faded. There was no genuine love between us. Not yet.

The next day, I called my friend Sarah and asked for the young lady's phone number. Sarah told me she'd get her permission first. I agreed. Later, she returned my call with the number. I called immediately.

"Hello?" Her strangely familiar voice brought back the intrigue I had felt the day before.

"Hi, this is Calvin. We met yesterday at the church? The guy with the handsome sons?" As though she didn't remember.

She, of course, played along with the ruse. "Oh yeah! I think I remember you."

Being done with the game, I began the conversation. "So I got your number from Sarah, as you know, and I was calling to just acquaint myself with you a little better."

"Okay, that sounds fine," she pleasantly responded.

After a few minutes of conversation, I asked her out.

Her response was surprising. "Well, I appreciate the invitation, but I'm not looking for a relationship right now. I don't mind being friends, but I'm not interested in anything deeper than that."

A challenge! I love a good challenge, but I was also interested in why she *wasn't* interested, so I pushed a little. "Really!? Well, honestly I'm not looking for a new friend. I have a lot of great friends and I'm not taking any more applications for new ones."

This surprised her. "Uh, really? Well, that's where I am and that's all I have to offer at this time."

The next response was one for the books. I don't know why I said it, but I'm sure glad I did.

"Is that so? Okay, Wendy, let's be real. You know you like me, you just don't want to admit it yet." It was a bold statement, but why not give it a shot?

Her response again was unexpected. "That is so arrogant!" She was shocked!

After a few more words, we ended the call and also possibly the potential for a great relationship. Love never occurred during that exchange. We never even got to the point of wanting to go out.

A few weeks later, I was out of town on business and decided to call her again.

"Hello?" she answered.

"Hey, this is Calvin. Thought I'd give you a call to say hi."

"Calvin, I thought you had kicked me to the curb?" she jokingly responded.

"Why? I thought we were friends! Friends don't have to talk

every day. Wait, you mean you *do* like me after all?" We both laughed and talked for a couple hours on the phone.

Afterward, I quietly thought to myself, *I'm going to marry her.*

It was at that point that I made the decision to be committed to this relationship, and that commitment was when love began. We never went a day after that without talking, and six months later we were married.

Love comes because you grow it, as opposed to falling into it, which releases the lovers from active participation. *Growing* in love means there must be an action on the part of the person making the commitment. There must be a decision to pledge to fulfill this person's need.

Just as in growing a plant, love requires nurturing, watering, and caring. This is a consistent process for as long as you want that plant around. No one just finds an orchid and carries it around without ever giving it any attention or care. You must know when to water, how much to water, and how much sunlight. People spend years learning how to care for plants yet spend very little time learning how to effectively love.

WHAT LOVE LOOKS LIKE

With that being said, I wish I could say the next few years of our marriage were all rainbows and bunny rabbits after such a romantic story. They were not! Because we are a blended family and both have older kids, there were quite a few growing pains as we were trying to continue to grow in love. We had to learn not only how to blend our lives as a couple, but also how to adapt to these new bonus kids who were simply passengers in our new marriage vehicle.

We have completely different parenting styles. Wendy is Caribbean, and according to her, it's her culture to have more of a disciplinarian/tough love approach. I was born in the country and had my share of whoopins, but I lean toward a less stringent way of child rearing.

Add to this the fact that my teenage son was not gracefully handling his teens and had his share of bad friends and bad behavior. Many times, I had to snatch him and exert parental dominance, but Wendy and I expressed discipline differently. This led to many painful and difficult arguments, which even now, after our son became an adult, still try to resurface.

Also, I was now the father of a little girl. A girl? I was only accustomed to boys! The boys were rugged and would laugh when I threw them in the air, and they wouldn't cry when I disciplined them. What was I supposed to do with a cute little girly girl?!

Then there were also differences in how we communicated. Many times, we asked ourselves, *What the heck were we thinking in marrying each other?* Bad attitudes, unnecessary egos, crossed boundaries, and arguments that seem to recur every few days took their toll on our marriage. It was exhausting!

Did we always *feel* good about each other? Absolutely not!

Did my wife's external beauty become less appealing each time we had an intense argument? Sadly, yes.

Did I disappoint her and give the impression that I was not the good man she thought I was? Undeniably yes!

Did we ever leave or even attempt to leave? Absolutely never!

We both understood we'd made a love decision. Our feelings would sometimes grow stale, but they would always return; most times even more intensely because we had triumphed together through tough times. We continually make the decision to reconcile because we realize the big picture of why we were married. We have decided to be committed. It is in that decision, and in our belief that the decision was good, that love has grown.

My college professor Dr. Claude Thompson and his lovely wife, Jo, were my unintended mentors in learning about love. They gave me this definition that I believe captures the essence of what love is: *Love is an intellectual decision we make to fulfill another person's legitimate need.* This was a transformative revelation to me. It showed me that I actually had some control in this love thing. This revelation showed me how to be a lifelong love partner.

Love is not in the feelings. The feelings are only a sign that love exists. Feelings are like the beautiful flowers that are an indication that there must be a healthy and well-nurtured root. Love is the root.

Many make this error, including Josh and Debbie. Being *in love* with someone is equated with the feelings of love. The root is the decision or commitment you've made to stay, irrespective of what you feel. So when a person says, "I'm not *in love* with you," they are really not understanding what love is. Love either exists or it doesn't.

This is difficult for a lot of people to grasp: to push through your feelings [the *in love* idea] and stay because you know [a decision] you love her, not because you feel like you love her. To persevere through arguments and disrespect; to reconcile and fight like hell when you really don't want to; to cry alone and reconcile together; to feel like walking out the door, but looking at the big picture; to go from disrespect to the highest regard—these are what successful marriages are made of. This is what love looks like.

WHERE LOVE COMES FROM

In order for love to be truly understood, it must first be demystified. I have always believed that in order to understand a particular thing, you must make it practical. You must take it from the ethereal to the real. You must figure out where love comes from.

Earlier we discussed love as a decision to commit to another's legitimate needs. Let's delve deeper into what that actually looks like. For starters, just saying the phrase "I love you" doesn't change who you are or how you feel about your significant other. Words are just that: an utterance of a subject, predicate, and direct object. "I love you." However, before the words are spoken, there should be something that prompts them. There should be some realized value you've seen in the person.

Debbie and Josh had all the feelings of love, but they never understood that feelings are not love and love is not a feeling. When they became disenchanted and the feelings began to wane, in their opinion, the love did also.

Here's how this love thing really works. The relationship guides the love, not the other way around. It is the relationship that determines the love and time, energy, disagreements, resolutions, fighting, making up, forgiving—all these elements are what relationships are made of. People in relationships go through things. They weather storms and decide to stay together and fight to make their relationship better.

> Love is the beautiful thing that emerges out of the mature soil your relationship is planted in.

Love is the natural outgrowth of this kind of relationship. Love is the beautiful thing that emerges out of the mature soil your relationship is planted in, and your commitment provides the rain that enables it to grow. That's where love comes from.

Unfortunately, a number of people don't experience love because they don't want to hang around for the hard work. It's easier to just depend on the feelings and then blame love that the feelings are no longer there.

This is the wrong way to experience a relationship. It's like watching a much-talked-about movie but leaving because you're lost in the first thirty minutes. If you really want to experience serious love and a long-lasting marriage, you must stay around till the end of the movie when the credits are rolling. You must wait until you get through the entire thing. Of course, this is barring extenuating circumstances like violence or antisocial behavior.

This is not a very popular look at love because it puts the responsibility in the hands of the lover, not in the hands of love. But after all, marriage ain't for punks! And love is not for the faint of heart. It is not for weaklings.

TYPES OF LOVE

As we look at how relationships create and sustain love, I must talk about different types of love. First, let me say that all love comes from the same source. It is all the same principle expressed in different ways. It is the same ocean with different tributaries branching from it. But at the root, love is just love—a deep and unfathomable source of emotion, commitment, and pleasure.

In my world, love comes from God. Everyone has to determine their own origin or source from which it comes, but it has to be from one source. I say this because however it is expressed, and irrespective of culture, race, gender, language, or any other thing that divides us, love feels the same to everyone. It has an identical thread of truth and commitment that runs through its all-encompassing fabric. No matter who you are or where you are from, it is a universal language.

You may call this language whatever you choose. The ancient Greeks called it *agape*. This is love as an eternal source. It is the universal source of all that is good. One unending source. One profound origin. It's just simple and pure love.

Now, there are many ways this love can be expressed. However, it's all driven by the relationship and your choices about how you plan to enact that love. For example, my relationship with my children directs how I choose to love them. The fact that I am their parent and I have a sense of responsibility to care for and protect them determines how I love them. I was there at their birth. I helped them to walk and taught them how to ride a bike. I was there when they needed help and guidance. Therefore, I have chosen to live in that space as protector, provider, teacher, and helper. That is my natural mindset toward my children, and that relationship defined the commitment or love I had for them.

Conversely, as romantic partners, a husband and a wife will have a different relationship, and that relationship will foster a different type of love. Because the focus and decision is to be involved in an intimate and sensual relationship, the focus and commitment are different than that of a parent.

For a husband and a wife, the goal is to be intimate partners, sharing life together.

No one stands in a parental space as an intimate partner. If they do, the romance dies. No wife or husband wants to cross those lines in a normal marriage. There must be lines of demarcation in the relationships so that the love can be expressed differently. Romantic partners speak differently to each other. They have different goals and desires, which are all determined by how they manage the relationship. They are lovers because the erotic love they have for one another is a result of the relationship they have fostered.

There are also brotherly or sisterly relationships, which brings about a different type of love. The filial relationship is one connected through the same parentage or even experiences that make you brothers or sisters. Regardless, this relationship is based on a caring that does not involve romance or eroticism. It is social and familial; not parental or erotic.

All these relationships engender different types of love, but all this love comes from one source: agape love. Divine love. Imagine it this way: A river is one body of water. Yet you can retrieve water from that one source for different usages. Some of it may go to a kitchen, where you will use it to drink and cook with. Some of it may go to the toilet, where you can use it to flush waste. And some of it may go to the shower, where you will bathe with it. It's all the same water but has different usages.

Not many people will use toilet water to cook with. They won't use shower water to wash their vegetables in. All the water has a different purpose, but it's all based on what you determine that purpose to be. You may drink from the toilet if you choose, but that is just nasty. No one wants to cross those boundaries.

Love is the same way. One source, different usages. All love is based on our relationships and how we have chosen to live those relationships. There is a practicality to love. It is not just an imaginary concept with no real significance. It grows out of relationships. So when a person says "I love you," there must be a relationship that has spawned that declaration. There must be some kind of connection that has been built so that the pronouncement of love is warranted.

Understanding the root of love and how it develops in your marriage will give you the strength to withstand the difficult times. Even when the feelings temporarily leave, you will know that there is something greater that has not left. You can hold on to the fact that the principle of love still remains.

LOVING THE WRONG WAY

That brings us to another point. I've heard many couples complain that their spouse will say "I love you," but they don't mean it. Here are a few of the complaints we've heard hurled at spouses:

- "If you loved, me, you wouldn't treat me the way you do."
- "Don't tell me you love me. You don't even know what that means."
- "Love me?! This is what you call love?"

When I look at these statements, I have to conclude that in most cases they are all true. They are definitely coming from a place where a spouse or partner feels they are not being loved the way they want to or need to be loved.

The sad reality is that the people making the complaints may not really know how they need to be loved. Many of us have not really sat down to think about this.

In their early years, Debbie and Josh thought they had a really good thing going. They both had finally found someone who would love them and fill the void that had been left by previous bad experiences. Sure, they understood that there would be an adjustment period, but they loved each other. That is, until they felt they didn't anymore.

But did love really leave? Were they no longer *in love*? I believe love was still there; they simply forgot or never learned how to grow it from their relationship. They felt love was what was guiding the relationships, when it was the other way around. The relationship was the fertile ground out of which their love should have grown.

In short, they were loving each other the wrong way. Why? Because they didn't understand what they needed in order to be loved.

Let me say that again: In order to be loved, a person must know what being loved looks like to them. They must understand themselves well enough to know that when their spouse does a certain thing, it makes them feel loved.

This is akin to asking someone to scratch your back but giving them no directions. You may be itching under your left shoulder blade, and they are peeling away at your lower back. But your partner should just know where you're itching, right? They should know this because they've seen you scratch your own back, or they should know you well enough to know where the itching shows up from time to time. *I shouldn't have to tell you what I need!*

Sounds ridiculous? Of course it's ridiculous. But so is trying to love someone when you have no idea what that looks like. There is a stark difference between loving the way you want to love and loving someone the way they need to be loved—caring for someone the way they need to be cared for.

There are many books and philosophies out there about the way we communicate love and our styles of loving. There have been many attempts to quantify how many there are. While I highly respect the incredible attempts to define love by a number of languages, the truth is there are as many ways to love and

receive love as there are personality types. Within these languages
of love there are many dialects.

For example, one couple I counseled struggled with a need for
intellectual stimulation. The entire problem in their relationship
was a lack of cerebral equality. She couldn't connect with him
about anything deeper than current events and superficial banter.
She didn't value his intellect, which led to her not valuing him.

She said he would often shut down and simply not talk to
her. A part of this was because he was a blue-collar worker and
a great provider. She was a PhD analyst and consultant. During
their conversations, she would talk rings around him, and he felt
completely powerless. They were intellectually mismatched. She
needed a man who could appeal to her mind. It was her way of
desiring to be loved.

A person's need to become self-actualized is another way to
show or receive love. A few couples I've talked to have struggled
with this. They feel their partner's desire to become a better person and achieve some kind of personal fulfillment is connected to
the success of their relationship. I've heard a few wives exclaim,
"You want to show me you love me? Get off your rear and do
something with your life—anything!"

For these women, the issue was not so much about making
a lot of money; they simply wanted their partner to achieve and
become their best. That is how they wanted to receive love. A
spouse may bring gifts, spend time with their partner, and talk
often, yet still be content with not achieving anything personally.
This is just not acceptable in a lot of marriages.

There are so many more love dialects, and each can be discovered only by actually discussing openly and honestly what each

person needs. Many frustrated spouses have come close to calling it quits because they can't seem to love their partner the way they need to be loved. To a large degree, this is often because the person lodging the complaint may not really know how to be or feel loved.

It takes a great deal of introspection and self-evaluation to know what actually gets your motor running. Discussing how we love is seldom an easy topic in relationships. Furthermore, we don't usually talk about it in our families. But these conversations are mandatory if you want to love your partner the *right way*. And the right way is how they desire to be loved.

Debbie and Josh are a shining example of two people who had no idea how they needed to be loved. Because Josh had dated so many women, he was in the habit of ending a relationship before he could find out. Debbie's emotional walls had prevented her from letting anyone in.

A naked moment was necessary between the two of them, where they actually reviewed what planted the seeds of love in the first place. They had to examine why their chance meeting was different from all the other encounters they'd had during dating. So once they stopped depending on their feelings and looked at the source of their love, they were able to reveal it to each other, and the journey to their healing could begin.

After removing all judgment and external distractions, Debbie felt safe to go first. She told him that he had pursued her and been interested in her mind. They had stayed up all night just talking about anything. She'd felt that nothing was prohibited, and she could be safe with him with all her flaws—in other words, she'd felt accepted. As the years progressed, she grew to feel that she had lost value in his eyes. The safety wasn't there anymore.

Through talking it out, she discovered that, for her, safety was the fertile soil in which the seed of love was planted. He had valued her and that was what she was missing. That was how she needed to be shown love. She needed to be appreciated and to feel that she was worth something to him, not disposable, as he had treated the other women he used to date.

That conversation lit a spark in Josh. It gave him a road map that he could follow to love her the right way. After he shared his heart and acknowledged her feelings, the new journey began.

Marriage is not easy, and conversations like these can be laborious. I'm not going to delude you into thinking that if you try these few brilliant tricks, your marriage will be trouble-free and a little heaven on earth. No! Marriage requires personal sacrifice, unconstrained giving, emotional nakedness, vulnerability, and a great deal of honest and sometimes painful communication.

None of this is easy. But no one said marriage is supposed to be a carefree walk in a manicured daisy-and-daffodil-laden park. Often that park is actually a rough and unsightly field of land mines. The two of you have to skip, sometimes unsuccessfully, through it until you know where all the bombs are planted. Once you know that, you can walk freely and comfortably on your marriage journey, hoping and praying your spouse doesn't plant any new mines without your knowing it.

All that being said, once you learn to dance through the minefield, there is a mixture of joy, adrenaline, and sheer excitement. You rejoice together because you both know the dangerous terrain. You both know how to avoid the pitfalls, and you rely on your partner to keep you safe. What once was an unknown field of hazards is now a familiar and comfortable garden where you both can frolic. You depend on each other to watch your backs and make sure you are protected because that now beautiful space can quickly become a battlefield again. You can't go through this field alone, and honestly, you don't want to. You need each other.

This is what love and marriage look like.

CHAPTER 10

Punks Don't Apologize

Lily and Marcus were the life of the party. That's how they were known among their friends. If Marcus told a joke, Lily would be his biggest cheerleader. People would wonder how two type A personalities could get along so well. And it seemed as though they did.

They had a mutual respect for what each person brought to the marriage. Marcus was the visionary. He could see the entire picture of what needed to happen. But he needed Lily to fill in the blanks and carefully determine what it would take and implement the necessary requirements to get there.

This is why their business was so successful. Marcus was the promoter and the face of their real estate house-flipping business. Lily kept up with the housing inventory and would monitor her husband, who had a tendency to want to purchase before the necessary due diligence. And this was the reason for the greatest challenge of their marriage.

Marcus saw an opportunity he could not refuse. He was

convinced this would be a home run and his instinct told him to go for it. So he stepped out of his lane and committed nearly half their savings to purchase a moderately sized commercial building to renovate and rent out space. It would create the continuous income they needed. This was their chance to get ahead; to make a big move that would take their business to the next level!

And it may have been a great idea—if he had talked to Lily first. She would have done what she customarily does: research the history and do the due diligence to see whether it was a sound and profitable venture. She would have found out what Marcus's cursory research did not. Lily later discovered there were some major issues with the area and also some hidden repairs needed, which inflated their expenses and cut into their profits substantially.

Marcus, however, wasn't really keen on asking for help. It was kind of his macho style. This is what a leader does, he felt. His philosophy was to ask for forgiveness rather than permission, and most of the time that worked out. He seemed to have nine lives and would always land on his feet.

It was just those few times when he didn't land on his feet that bothered Lily. Those times when asking for forgiveness never really happened. Apologizing was about as easy for him as pulling his own teeth. Only in a few cases could Lily even remember him humbling himself to say, "I'm sorry."

What was an impulsive business failure quickly became a marriage issue. Of course, there had been other decisions she didn't agree with, but they always managed to work it out. *Working it out* meant he would mess up and she would catch the error and fix it. He would realize she'd caught the problem, and they would continue without ever talking about it.

This was their way, and it kept them moving along, with Lily carrying the emotional weight of the unexpressed conflict. For Marcus, it wasn't necessary to say the words "I'm sorry," right? They both knew they were good, and as long as the marriage was moving along, what was the big deal? All's well that ends well.

But was the marriage moving along? Was everything well? Or was it just ending well for him? It seemed as though Marcus was moving along fine, while Lily was starting to feel she was the one emotionally holding the marriage together. It wasn't that he was a horrible person or that he was unkind to her, but this subconscious disregard for her feelings was accumulating some serious indifference on her part.

TWO TOUGH WORDS

I have seen so many couples who could have a thriving and happy marriage, but one or sometimes both parties refuse to apologize. They will not back down. They make excuses for their behavior, circumvent the topic, throw the blame back on the offended spouse, or even make comparisons of wrongdoing with comments like, "You do the same thing!" But they refuse to apologize.

Sometimes a person may feel there is no real reason to formally apologize. I've heard some spout the viewpoint, "Don't apologize, just do better!"

While I get the philosophy behind that statement, it doesn't really work. There is a process to reconciliation. There is a way to resolve a disagreement so that both parties are cleansed of the negative emotions that accompany the conflict. Feelings like anger, indifference, disappointment, and fear can be brought to light and resolved through understanding how to reconcile. Apologizing is the first step in the process.

But let's talk about why some people find it so difficult to say "I'm sorry." Why is it that some people can only bite their lip and spit out muted mumblings that have a faint resemblance to the words? Others fuel their apology with so much sarcasm and rudeness that even when it's said, it has lost its authenticity and healing power.

This resistance to uttering an actual apology is often caused by fear. Some would argue differently, but for people like Marcus, the thought of seeming vulnerable was terrifying. It made him feel weak and emasculated to apologize. Admitting wrong was like groveling.

All this stemmed from his personal history. He had picked up the idea that a man doesn't kowtow or subjugate himself. As a man myself, I understand the sentiment. Society and the media often paint that unrealistic picture of what a man looks like. But I also realize that when you're in a relationship with a loving and understanding spouse, there is a huge difference between humbling oneself to a trusting partner and bending to someone who will kick you when you're down.

Pride and stubbornness both find their roots in fear. I believe many of us are terrified of being found out. We are scared of letting our guard down and showing even our most trusted loved ones the fact that we don't know it all. We are not always perfect and we do fail. So we keep our mistakes to ourselves and talk things through in our head, because we know at the very least we can trust ourselves.

HOW TO APOLOGIZE

The idea that there is a right way to apologize I'm sure is foreign to many. Just say "I'm sorry," right? Well, most of the time, a good apology is not about the actual words as much as the intentions behind those words. It's about whether the words are coming from a sincere place. Whether the words are only a prelude to a true acknowledgment of the pain that was caused or the damage that was done. Because if there is a sincere understanding, then there can be honest communication, and if there is communication, then there can be a viable resolution.

A Positive Environment

The first thing needed for an effective apology to happen is a positive and accepting environment. Often, a person will not come close to an apology if they feel there is the slightest chance that their vulnerability will be crushed by the listener. That's why some will cover an apology with sarcasm or indifference. The feeling is that if the apology is not naked, then the person offering it can't be hurt as badly. If they aren't completely exposed, then they can't be damaged.

Sometimes, when the potential receiver is positioned in a way that shows he or she is impatiently waiting for an apology, they have created the perfect environment for it not to happen, or at least not to happen sincerely. I can't count the times I've tried to arbitrate an argument between two heated individuals and one will eventually eke out a half-hearted apology. Immediately, the receiver spouts off, "See? He didn't mean it!"

The moment is completely destroyed in that instant. The environment is not conducive for either party to be genuine and honest about their feelings. They are both already in battle mode and have their defenses up, afraid of being seen as the weak one in the relationship. To create a proper setting for a successful apology, each person must remove the enemy mentality. Meaning, they need to stop treating their spouse as the problem. They must understand that in marriage, not winning does not mean you're losing. It means you're finding resolution.

It is a huge thing for a person to apologize, so the receiver must let the giver know that it's safe to say what needs to be said. Posturing as though you're owed something is not the way to do it. Remember that your gestures and expressions are important in how you communicate your feelings. Nowhere is this more evident than when your partner has offended you or made an error of some kind. You must make the environment such that a person feels safe to admit wrong.

This may not be a popular way to look at the situation, because when many people feel they are right, they want it to be known they are right. They want to feel justified or given some credit. But this is where maturity has to take over. This is where you have to dig deep and force yourself to focus on resolution rather than justification, if your marriage is going to thrive.

A Willing Heart

Next, the desire to apologize has to be evident. Often people don't apologize simply because they don't want to. They have lost the desire to care about whether they have offended their partner. As a result, a person may carelessly utter the words "I'm sorry," but will not give a flip as to whether their partner likes it or not.

A person loses the desire to reconcile when they have lost respect for or have devalued their partner. When you value anything, you want to take care of it and protect it. It's the same with your spouse. When you have respect for them, you want to see the conflict ended and you have a deep desire to find resolution, because you want peace between the two of you.

Marcus genuinely loved Lily and valued her. He just didn't know he was hurting her. He didn't realize his actions were showing her disrespect. He had become so caught up in being *the man* and running the business that he forgot that his business partner was his partner in life.

This is actually why Lily tolerated his impetuous behavior. She knew he loved her, and he often showed that in a number of ways. He had just become so myopic in his work that he'd edged her out.

When a spouse truly wants to reconcile and their partner knows they have a desire to do so, it is easier to get to that place of resolution. When someone knows you care about them, half the battle is over. From there, it's just a matter of learning how to love them the way they need to be loved.

A Receptive Attitude

The third element in setting the stage for an apology is knowing how to receive the confession. When a spouse finally gets to the point where they are showing their heart and the desire to reconcile, and then they say the words "I'm sorry" with sincerity and vulnerability, the absolute last thing they want to hear is, "Yeah, you should be sorry!"

I've seen many apologies go wrong because the receiver just dropped the ball, making comments such as, "I know you're sorry…a sorry excuse for a husband." Or the just as painful to hear, "Sorry didn't do the wrong, you did!" Or, "I don't need your apology!"

Other responses are not as scathing, such as "But why did you do it?" Or, "What were you thinking?"

Now, the first few responses are obviously just wrong. Their apparent intention is to kick the person when they are down and make them grovel. For the record, those are the perfect responses if you aren't finished arguing yet, and you want to continue in battle until someone is destroyed. (I don't recommend such an approach.)

The latter responses are a probe into what was behind the actions that caused the need to apologize. Wanting to know what caused the problem is fine, but the timing is completely off. Furthermore, these are questions that no one who has ever done something stupid could actually answer. I mean, if you knew why you made mistakes, you wouldn't make them, right? Obviously, you weren't thinking about *not* doing the deed. You were thinking it was either the right thing to do or you could get away with it.

Let's look at these negative responses a little closer. When a person perceives that an apology is insincere, their response may be laced with sarcasm or defensiveness. This is completely under-standable, especially when you feel someone is not revealing their heart or that they're just trying to end the conflict with a limp con-fession. But this is where marriage grit has to show up. Irrespec-tive of whether you feel the apology is heartfelt, your response to it will determine whether the door will be open to reconciliation—or closed. Your spouse's weak apology is their anemic call for a cease-fire. Use that attempt to open the door further.

When a person apologizes, either sincerely or halfheartedly, this is your time to be graceful and grateful. This is the time to take the high road and see that the goal is to bring clarity and rec-onciliation to the situation. The proper thing is to understand it took a lot to apologize, express that fact, and then simply say with all sincerity, "I accept your apology."

Now, understand that by accepting the apology, you're not accepting the wrongful act. You're accepting the offender's acknowledgment that they made a mistake. This is why your response should not be, "It's okay," or, "Don't worry about it." Because it's not okay. There was some bad thing that happened. Additionally, you want the offender to worry enough to correct or repair the error. But accepting the apology is simply saying, "I accept that you see where you went wrong."

We will talk about what forgiveness looks like in the next chapter. Now, let's look a little deeper into apology types.

APOLOGY TYPES

Lily was furious about Marcus's hasty decision—one that could have cost them a great deal of money and time, if she wasn't such an excellent fixer. But outside of what seemed to be their constant work schedule, she longed for a time when they could actually talk this through. She needed the emotional weight to be lifted. She needed Marcus to be her hero, just this once.

He sensed what she needed, and he wanted to give her that emotional reprieve, so he thought he would do something nice for her. He booked a trip for the two of them. He wanted to show her how much he appreciated her and how valuable she was to him. He planned a romantic dinner, scheduled a babysitter, and made everything perfect. Then, at dinner, he sprung the surprise.

She was happy about the trip because they needed to get away, but he still missed his opportunity to connect with her. In fact, he could have saved himself a great deal of money and time if he had just been proactive in apologizing. That's all she wanted. She wanted him to recognize how his actions affected her. She wanted his heart—and then the vacation.

Marcus is not unlike many people who are unskilled in resolving conflict. I'm sure when most people apologize, they don't consider that there are ways to do it.

Let's examine the three types of apologies.

Proactive

The first is the proactive apology. This is the ideal confession of wrongdoing. To be proactive is to be preemptive or to be the first one to act. When you see you've done something wrong, an apology never needs to be requested. You give it because you recognize the truth and you want to resolve the issue as quickly as possible.

If I could get more couples to proactively apologize, they would avoid many hours of grief and frustration. This is what Wendy and I call *rushing to reconcile*. With a proactive apology, you don't wait until the wrong is discovered; you rush toward the challenge.

This goes against our natural way of doing things. When a person encounters something threatening, the natural response is to run as far from it as possible. For example, when you touch a hot surface, the natural response is to flinch and withdraw. It's what any reasonable person would do.

But when it comes to marriage, I believe firmly you should do the opposite. When there is a conflict, a proactive mindset says you should run toward the problem. Apologize for your part in it and then seek to reconcile by any means necessary. But the acknowledgment of your wrong has to be first.

I have often heard couples balk against this counsel. They refuse to apologize for anything they had *no part* in. I agree with that for the most part. It's just that most of the problems in marriages can be traced to both parties. Now, of course there are exceptions to the rule. Some spouses may just lose their minds and commit terrible offenses against their spouse because of some previous trauma or the like. But in most cases, for most marriages, there is mutual culpability. When that's the case, you must proactively be responsible for whatever your contribution to the problem was.

Let's get back to Marcus and Lily. He was responsible for making the decision to buy the building. This is where what I call *Marriage Math* applies. He may have been 100 percent responsible, or he may have been only 95 percent responsible. Lily may have been 5 percent responsible because he's been impulsive before and she never checked him on it. She may have not wanted him to feel bad or didn't want to seem like she was doing his job.

Now, this is not blaming the victim. Again, Lily may have no culpability in the mistake; that's for them to determine. But let's just imagine she was 5 percent responsible. Marcus is 100 percent answerable for his 95 percent of his personal and irresponsible input in the decision. Lily is 100 percent responsible for her 5 percent input of not checking him in the past.

Let me outline further just what this looks like. I want to make sure you completely understand how this works. The following are qualities of a proactive apology:

- First, the person sincerely speaks the words "I'm sorry," without having to be provoked or prodded.

- They admit their error and take personal responsibility for their part in the wrong without mentioning what anyone else did.
- They apologize even if the receiver is not aware of the problem. They will make their partner aware of the error and try to clean it up, because they want complete honesty and openness.
- They desire to end the issue before it gets out of hand. They're in damage control mode. *If we handle this quickly, we can get back to a successful relationship.*
- Lastly, they are realistic about consequences and are willing to face whatever they are because the goal is to reconcile.

Reactive

The next type of apology is the reactive apology. It's called reactive because it's normally a reaction to the realization that something has occurred. It may be a sincere revelation or a falsified one, but the apology comes after the issue has been revealed and confronted. Often, this is an apology that is given because it is requested. It may be sincere or insincere.

For example, Marcus's philosophy was to ask for forgiveness instead of permission, which is the essence of the reactive apologizer. This person will admit wrong only when cornered. This is like the spouse who is caught cheating red-handed. The next words from his mouth are obvious: "This is not what it looks like," or, "I can explain." It's a reaction to something that has already been discovered.

The very reason an apology is so powerful in a relationship is that it breaks down walls. When someone expresses sincere regret, the confession literally strips away pretense and pride and lets the hearer know that the offender realizes the gravity of their actions. They understand the pain they've caused and want to do whatever is in their power to heal the hurt. It's like throwing yourself at the mercy of another person.

This is most powerful when it's unsolicited and unprovoked. A person's sincerity shines forth boldly when they realize their own role in the issue and transparently reveal remorse, without excuses. Even if the wrong cannot be corrected, it gives some comfort when an injured party realizes their mistake and is willing to make restitution.

The reactive apology takes that vulnerability away. It is a solicited response, one that is requested. As such, it may be more challenging to forgive or recover from, because the sincerity is always in question. The common response to a reactive apology is, *Are you apologizing because you are genuinely sorry or because you were caught?* More often than not, it's the latter.

Marcus, in purchasing the property without consulting his wife, was holding out in hopes that the whole thing would work out. He believed that his decision was a sound one. Furthermore, when Lily finally found out about it and realized just what a great decision it was, any apology would be insignificant. Or at least, the apology would be a minimal thing that he could sweep under the rug of his colossal success. Unfortunately, things didn't work out that way; not by a long shot!

This is what often happens when we make ill-advised decisions in relationships. We pray for the best results. And if things go as planned, we'll handle the negligible consequences and eke out an apology. It's a part of who we are as flawed humans. We all have the tendency to make unwise decisions and expect great results.

I have talked to many husbands and wives who harmlessly flirt while out with the boys or the girls. They don't expect anything detrimental to come out of it. They'll feel good about the fact that they are still attractive or that they can catch the eye of a stranger.

So they may casually flirt for a moment just to feel good about themselves, and then if the conversation gets a little too hot, they'll back out of the quick romantic liaison before it goes too far. They think, *No harm, no foul.* That is, until a friend of their spouse sees them in the midst of their flirtation and reports it, or a text or social media post is discovered. Then they have to apologize because they were caught.

There are, however, instances when a reactive apology can be sincere. For example, when a spouse is unaware they are offending their partner. This is pretty common in relationships. Someone will be completely perturbed about a certain behavior and will not communicate it until the frustration shows up in their actions. Then, when that unknown mistake is brought to the offender's attention, they react to that knowledge with an apology. This is a sincere reactive apology.

When I was a bachelor, I had my own guy habits, which were fine for me. While I was neat, I wasn't pristine. I didn't always pick up my clothes. It was normal for me to come home after a long day at work and literally walk out of my clothes and to my bed. I'd pick them up the next morning.

This kind of behavior was fine the first few weeks of my marriage. Wendy allowed quite a few things to pass. I now see it was my orientation. I was just learning the ropes, so there was a lot of grace shown toward me. But after months of me not getting the message from seeing her pick up my clothes, she had to not so delicately bring it to my attention.

I would have continued the behavior had she not informed me. It didn't bother me to leave a trail of fashionable debris in my path as I went to the bed. But what was not a big deal early on became a big deal when it never stopped. I was happy to apologize and correct the behavior once I knew about it. Besides, it was a small thing to do for everyone to be happy.

Resolution makes everyone happy, and apologizing is the first step in that process. Someone wittily coined the cute phrase "Happy wife, happy life." In our home we choose to expand the joy and say, "Happy spouse, happy house."

Let's look at the elements of a reactive apology.

A sincere reactive apology:

- Is offered when a person is not willing to risk the relationship over pride or selfishness.
- Willingly desires to make restitution for the wrongdoing when it's brought to their attention.

An insincere reactive apology:

- Is given when the offender is caught and has no other option but to apologize.
- May be given when the offender just wants to abruptly end the conversation.

Inactive

The last apology type is an *inactive apology*. This happens when a person wants to avoid conflict or discussion, but they want it to be known that they are, in fact, remorseful. They don't want to have a long conversation about it or talk about feelings, so they just do better or perform some kindness without ever discussing the issue. This is not actually saying "I'm sorry," but by doing something kind, they are hoping this compensates for having to say the words.

Marcus was the quintessential expert at this, and if Lily hadn't been the keen observer and operations manager that she was, he would have gladly continued his course of not confronting his wrong. He felt they both knew he *may have* made a mistake. Why discuss it? He would rather just shower her with gifts to show that he understood his error.

This is actually a cowardly way to attempt resolving an issue in your relationship. While giving gifts and acts of service are a necessary part of caring for one another, their efficacy is not realized when a person does not verbally acknowledge the possible hurt that has been caused by bad behavior.

The inactive apology is actually a very selfish way to maintain a relationship. It takes the option of dealing with the issue away from the offending party. Whenever Marcus made decisions without consulting with his partner/wife, and then acted as though nothing had happened, he was taking Lily's power away. Each time he did it, he was chipping away at her ability and right to have an equal say in the relationship. He was making the decision that the issue was not going to be discussed, and he acted accordingly. The message was sent to her that discussing his mistake was off-limits. And if she chose to bring it up regardless, he would further shut down.

To cross the barrier the offender has built and talk about it anyway is never easy. You never know what you're going to encounter, so in most cases I've experienced, the partner simply leaves the topic alone and goes on. Besides, you can tell the person is apologetic because of the kind or nice treatment.

This, of course, is not a sustainable condition in which to live and grow a marriage. The frustration and dissatisfaction will continue to grow with each unresolved issue. Inactive apologies are the absolute worst way to apologize because they don't go very far toward bringing honesty and vulnerability to the relationship.

Sometimes a spouse may inactively apologize because they don't feel safe making mistakes in their marriage. They are afraid of their spouse's responses. I've seen couples hide their mistakes because they feel that if they apologize, the response will be worse than the actual offense. Therefore, when a mistake is evident, they just treat their spouse as though they're making it up to them.

At the root of the inactive apology is a serious fear of appearing vulnerable or weak. In Marcus's case, he was simply too proud to admit he was wrong. He thought that admitting his mistakes would somehow diminish who he was. It would lessen his personal power. What he didn't understand was that by retaining his power, he was at the same time taking Lily's power away. He was simultaneously draining her emotionally and placing the weight of their unresolved issues on her shoulders.

In their case, she had to be the one to openly tell him how his behavior was affecting her. And because he did genuinely love her, his love outweighed his arrogance. He didn't want to lose his wife at the expense of his pride. Arrogance has little place in a healthy and emotionally vulnerable marriage. Both parties must trust in their spouse's ability to love them through their mistakes and failures.

Here are the qualities of an inactive apology:

- Often a person may be too prideful or cowardly to speak the words.
- A person may not feel as though the words "I'm sorry" are necessary.
- A person does not want to feel vulnerable and transparent.
- The apology may come from a fear of not being accepted.

In summary, when a person says "I'm sorry," here is what they're saying: *I understand what I've done wrong and I am making efforts to turn away from that thing.* They will also try their best never to repeat that same behavior.

When an apology is given, the words "I accept your apology" should be uttered without reciprocal criticism or grandstanding. This is not the time for foolishness. This is an opportunity to begin on the road to reconciliation. This is a time to open the door and be vulnerable and honestly hear each other's hearts.

CHAPTER 11

Forgiveness Ain't
for Punks

Forgiveness is probably the most challenging thing to do in a relationship. This was definitely the case with Gena and Ian. After twelve years of marriage, you would think they had figured out how to get along with each other. But it seemed as though they'd been on a downward spiral for at least ten of those years.

After only a short time into the marriage, Ian reconnected with an old girlfriend on social media. It was a pleasant reunion, and even one that he shared with Gena. She saw all the messages and was assured that it was only a platonic reunion, so she soon forgot about the connection.

But when she and Ian started to have some serious arguments having to do with her not wanting to have a baby yet, he started sharing those intimate details with his ex. Social media connections soon evolved into meeting for a quick lunch during work hours. That turned into a dinner meeting—and a two-month-long affair.

It wasn't long before the secret exposed itself. Ian's ex felt scorned when he tried to break off the relationship. He told her he wanted his marriage and the affair was a mistake. In retaliation, Gena received an anonymous call from his ex revealing their secret affair.

Ian made no excuses and did not try to justify his actions. He took full responsibility and begged profusely for his marriage. They had counseling and were on the road to recovery. For the next year, Ian felt things were going well. He had his family back. That is, until he started receiving calls again from the ex. Even though he revealed everything to Gena, she didn't believe he had completely cut ties, which was one of the requirements of their reconciliation.

Gena felt betrayed. It was as though she had believed a lie. His apology and contrition were just a scam, she thought. Could she even forgive him? Could her trust be restored?

For many couples, this is the one deal breaker in their marriage. If someone cheats, it's over. To the contrary, I've seen couples recover from infidelity. I've counseled couples through the murky waters of this marriage death sentence and have helped them receive a pardon from each other and healing for their relationship.

Apologizing for the wrong is only the first step. The most difficult part is forgiveness.

TWO DEFINITIONS

The ability to forgive or absolve someone of the wrongs they've committed toward you is no less than a divine act. It requires a deep desire to confront the issue and find out how it can be removed from your marriage.

Here is how I define forgiveness: *the act of releasing a person from the penalty or pressure of our personal judgment and treating them as though they had never wronged you.*

Now, read that again slowly, because that is a hugely powerful statement—one that is almost impossible to achieve on our own. In fact, if a person is truly going to forgive, there must be dependence on something much greater than themselves. There is actually an unseen power in forgiveness. The amount of strength and moral courage required to absolve another person of the wrong they have committed is almost superhuman.

Having someone disappoint you or act in a way that truly offends you can be devastating. Trust is not always easy to come by, so when someone as close as a spouse breaches that trust, it can be heartrending and very hard to recover from. Nevertheless, it is possible.

I must dispel a myth at this point. There is a prevailing idea that in order to forgive, a person must submit themselves to a lower position than the offender. They must acquiesce in such a manner that they are exposing themselves to more abuse. This could not be further from the truth. Forgiveness is not an act of weakness. On the contrary, it is an act of incredible strength and tenacity. It requires maturity and is a sure way to preserve your personal power as you begin the healing process.

> **Forgiveness is not an act of weakness. On the contrary, it is an act of incredible strength and tenacity. It requires maturity and is a sure way to preserve your personal power as you begin the healing process.**

Let's look at another definition of forgiveness. According to Merriam-Webster.com "to forgive" is "to cease to feel resentment against (an offender); PARDON . . . [to] forgive one's enemies or to give up resentment of or claim to requital." Lastly it means "to grant relief from payment."

When we delve deeper into those words, there are two components that stand out if we are going to forgive.

The first component has to do with releasing the feeling of resentment toward the person who offended you. There is an emotional weight that a person carries when they've been offended or wronged. It starts with the heartbreak or hurt. I've always thought the word "heartbreak" was interesting because, medically, there isn't a literal crack or fracture in the muscular organ when we are betrayed, but that does feel like the most appropriate way to describe the painful emotions attached to that betrayal.

This painful feeling is the reason people often lash out at the offender. It's why many find it difficult to move forward in the relationship when forgiveness is required. It can be a seemingly unbearable pain, and you would almost believe there is a physical break in the cardiac chamber. Many people find it just too difficult to get beyond that feeling of hurt.

But here's the truth: The pain you experience after a betrayal or a wrong is not a physical response. It is a feeling. Yes, it is an incredibly painful feeling, but a feeling, nevertheless. And all feelings have the ability to remain or leave based on what we choose to do with them.

You may believe you can no longer trust your spouse because all the time, energy, and resources you've invested in the marriage have been compromised by a foolish act. These are real and powerful emotions that must be realized and dealt with in the process of forgiveness. However, at the end of the day, it must be understood that feelings are always under your control.

Whether it's grief, anger, sadness, frustration, or any other myriad of reactions, they do not exist without your being connected to them. They are a part of you; hence, you have the ability to regulate their intensity. It's not an easy thing to do, but it is possible and necessary.

The other component of forgiveness has to do with the direction of your feelings or what you want to be done because of what your partner did. The ancient Greek word for forgiveness is *aphesis*, which literally means to release from bondage or imprisonment or to pardon sins. This has to do with what you want to happen to the person who wronged you.

Often someone may be hurt, yet he or she doesn't want harm to come to the offender. They don't want punishment or retribution. They just want an acknowledgment of the pain and want it to stop. This is what Gena felt when she first learned of Ian's infidelity. She was devastated, but still loved him and wanted to know just how to get through it.

Then there are those who feel that relieving the hurt isn't good enough. They want judgment. They want the offender to feel pain. They want revenge and they want it quickly.

I can frequently tell if a couple can get beyond infidelity in their marriage based on this point. Are we dealing with hurt feelings, which can be overcome? Or are we dealing with a person who wants judgment? Do they want to see blood?

In order to truly forgive, these emotions have to be uncovered and dealt with. It has to be determined what the offended party actually wants now that the offense has happened. Do you just want the pain to stop? Do you want a change in behavior and healing to begin with a mutual understanding of how much devastation has occurred because of the actions? Or do you want someone to pay?

When Gena found out that Ian and his ex were still having some contact, the desire for judgment kicked in. It was no longer a matter of Ian making a mistake. She felt this had become a bad habit, and to indulge his behavior was destroying her from the inside out. She didn't want Ian to confuse her meekness for weakness. She had forgiven him for his infidelity and was actually on the road to making the marriage work before he resumed contact with his ex. To Gena's mind, just when the healing had begun, he ripped off the bandage and reopened the same wound. But this time it was even more painful because she felt disrespected.

Their marriage became a war zone with missiles of painful emotion fired carelessly at one another. This made forgiveness even more difficult. Gena had forgiven him once, which wasn't easy, and now she had to revisit the same issue as before. Could even this be forgiven?

I believe it can. Gena and Ian's marriage was not beyond redemption. There had been some serious damage caused by his behavior, but even with that, there was still a chance for healing and reconstruction of their marriage—if they could go through the right process.

RESPONSIBLE FORGIVENESS

As Gena and Ian sat in front of me, it seemed like a hopeless situation. He had committed the cardinal sin in marriage. Yet they were sitting in front of me. They were looking for an answer. Whether they were completely convinced that their marriage could recover at that point was irrelevant. They were making the effort, and that is where the healing begins.

The pathway to complete forgiveness is not an easy one, but it is possible. The offender and the offended party both must understand that it will take complete authenticity and vulnerability to get to a place where they can trust again. While that will be a long and arduous journey, it is movement. And where there is movement, there can be progress.

Understanding what forgiveness looks like is the key to reconstructing a marriage after a major offense. At this point, I tell couples they must look at the offense as an enemy to their marriage. This is something that happened to both of them. Even though it may have been perpetrated by one of them, they both have been affected.

Gena was affected because her world was broken. They were on the way to becoming another failed marriage statistic. She had lost confidence in the man she loved. *Do I really even know him anymore? Has he been lying to me our entire marriage? What about all the times he said "I love you"—did he even mean it?*

She lost confidence in herself and began to doubt her own value. *Am I good enough? Was there something I could have done to prevent this? Maybe if I lost weight or was more adventurous in the bedroom, it would have helped.*

Believe it or not, Ian was also affected. He carried the guilt of what he had done to Gena. He heard her crying in the shower and it tore him apart. He noticed her energetic light had been diminished. She didn't want him to touch her. He felt the weight of her pain.

He was also angry at himself. *How could I have been so stupid? I'm ruining everything we have worked for. The time with my ex wasn't even that great! What is wrong with me? I'm embarrassed and ashamed of myself.*

Both parties were experiencing their own set of emotions, fears, and disappointments. They were both severely affected by one person's actions. As difficult as this is, they must look at the infidelity as an enemy of the relationship and not as an attachment to Ian. Of course, he is the perpetrator. He is the one who cheated and this must be acknowledged and understood, but in order to heal the marriage, the issue, not the spouse, is the enemy.

Many couples can't get beyond this point. They can't seem to separate the issue from the person. In my experience, the only way to make that happen is to commit to open communication.

As we talked, Ian shared that his father had cheated on his mother. As a young boy, he saw the turbulence and difficulty they both experienced in trying to overcome his dad's errors in growing up. Ian had even vowed he would never be unfaithful to his wife. But he also really admired his dad, and although he loathed what he did to his mom, he still wanted to be like him. Although Ian didn't approve of his father's behavior, he did find he possessed his dad's charisma and charm. This is what led him down the same road as his father.

Gena's understanding of this gave her some insight into realizing why Ian continually responded that he didn't know why he did it. With this, she was able at least to begin to separate him from his transgression. The long journey had just begun for them, and I needed them to travel it together.

When someone is offended, the first response is to get away from the person who did them wrong. I've often heard couples say, "We're taking some time away from each other to heal."

In my experience, most times this doesn't work. Although I do believe healthy marriages should occasionally have their own private time, when a marriage has been injured by the acts of one or both, they need to come together, not separate. This especially is the time to be in each other's space to find solutions and healing.

Think of it this way: When someone is burned, that person withdraws from the heat. It is a natural reaction. If a person is being pelted by hail, they quickly find shelter. The normal human response to hurt, pain, or injury is to retreat. No one in their right mind runs toward pain and misery. You want to get as far from it as possible.

Forgiveness urges a person to fight against that normal human response. Instead of retreating, forgiveness requires us to confront the challenge and find resolutions. It opposes the desire to get away for self-preservation and instead runs toward the injury to quickly find a remedy.

> Instead of retreating, forgiveness requires us to confront the challenge and find resolutions. It opposes the desire to get away for self-preservation and instead runs toward the injury to quickly find a remedy.

TWO PERSPECTIVES: THE FORGIVEN

Here is what the actual act of forgiving a person looks like. It must be viewed from two perspectives: that of the wrongdoer and that of the offended. Both parties have a huge part to play if there is a chance at reconciliation, especially for infidelity in marriage.

Let me say that again: The weight of healing a marriage should never rest on one person.

To start, the forgiven spouse has the responsibility of

understanding that he or she wants resolution quicker than the forgiver. Most people who are seeking pardon for an act that they're ashamed of want to forget that act as soon as possible. They want to move on and let bygones be bygones. Besides, if the apology has been given and forgiveness has been granted, what else is there to talk about?

Actually, there's a lot more to talk about after forgiveness has been granted. It is only after the conversation occurs and the issue has been placed on the table that real communication can begin. Once a spouse consents to forgive, then the damage has to be discussed. Has trust been broken? What needs to be done to rebuild? Have there been physical consequences of the actions? Are there strings that need to be cut and outside relationships that need to be severed?

These are all issues that need to be discussed when both parties have decided that their relationship is going to survive this challenge. And the one receiving forgiveness must be patient during this process. They must understand it takes a tremendous amount of strength for their spouse to forgive—yet even with that, the memories don't leave.

The act of saying "You're forgiven" is the first step, not the last. It's only saying "We can still have our relationship, but something has definitely changed. We've altered our marriage. We cannot go back to the way it was; rather, we have to find out what we have now." With that in mind, what new boundaries have been established? What new sensitivities now exist because of hurt feelings, embarrassment, and new fears?

The worst thing a forgiven person can do is rush the process. There will be times when the offended spouse wants to talk about it. They may randomly bring up the topic and just want to clear the air because they are having an insecure moment. The forgiven person has to understand this, be patient, be caring, and realize this is part of the healing process. Besides, none of this would have been necessary had the offense never occurred.

This is not a quick fix. It is not a microwave solution. It takes time, patience, and tenacity for the forgiven person to hang in there and sometimes even take a beating so that their partner can heal from the issue. There are no timetables; no predetermined schedules as to when someone should *get over it*.

Ian had already gone through a great deal of his own personal healing before Gena found out about what he had done. He had processed his wrong, decided it was not worth it, and made the conscious decision to end the affair. He had already experienced his personal resolution. As such, he was much further along in the healing process than Gena.

It would be completely unfair and unreasonable for him to expect her to move up to his place of healing. She just found out, through his ex, and she simply had to take some time to get to a level of comfort and understanding about the situation.

This is where a lot of couples fail. They don't realize that the timelines for healing are unequal during a period of forgiveness.

No one can determine how long a person should take to get over an offense. Many offenders will get frustrated that the issue has to be discussed again. I cannot count how many times I've heard a spouse come back out of frustration with the statement "I said *I'm sorry*, now can't we just move on?"

This is an understandable posture to take for someone who feels bad about their own actions. Each time it's discussed, they are painfully reminded of their thoughtless decision. They feel embarrassed to have to go over the same details again. So rushing their partner to heal is their way of protecting themselves. It's self-ish, but reasonable.

But saying the words "I'm sorry" does not encapsulate the complete reconciliation of the issue. The offender's job is not to instruct their partner on how to heal. In fact, however long it takes, the offender has to cement it in their mind that if they are willing to see the relationship work, they must also be willing to wait for it.

TWO PERSPECTIVES: THE FORGIVER

The forgiver also has a responsibility in the reconciliation process. Gena had to realize she needed to take time to absorb the information, process it, and grieve through it. This cannot be scheduled or forced. If a couple is going to heal from a challenge like theirs, both parties must have sufficient time to rid themselves of or heal from the complex emotions brought on by the issue.

That being said, the forgiver must also understand that healing from an emotional wound and dispensing punishment to the perpetrator are two completely different things. It's natural to want the offender to pay for his or her crimes. The forgiver wants not only emotional healing but also punitive damages.

I've heard so many hurt individuals say, "I want him to feel the same thing I feel." While I understand the sentiment, in most cases, what the hurt person wants is for their partner to empathize with their pain. *Understand what you've done to me!* The need for retribution is never a healthy way to handle a marital problem.

In fact, this is what leads a lot of hurt spouses to go out and have their own affair. They think, *Now you understand how I feel.* However, I have never seen a situation where a retaliatory affair causes the newly offended party to say "I now understand." In truth, it has nothing to do with understanding. A responsive affair is a knee-jerk reaction to a painful situation and is a certain and decisive step toward ending the marriage altogether.

Even though a time limit cannot be put on how long it takes for a person to heal, there are definitely some boundaries in regard to *how* you heal. If a person truly still wants their marriage after their heart has been broken, it's important to make sure they don't do anything that will exacerbate the problem. And nothing can do that more quickly and effectively than retaliating with the same offense.

ALL-INCLUSIVE FORGIVENESS

One of the greatest fears in forgiving someone is whether they will take advantage of your mercy. One of the main questions people ask during this healing process is, "Will they see me as a pushover and then do the same thing again? I already trusted them with my heart and I was disappointed. I don't want to do that again."

I wish I could predict the future and assure spouses as to whether they should expose themselves to hurt again. But there is absolutely no way to know. We are all flawed and error-prone humans. I don't ever remember speaking to a person who was unfaithful to their partner who said, "I knew I was going to hurt my spouse!"

Most everyone is surprised by their own actions. Only in a few cases have I encountered people who actually set out to hurt their spouse. It's normally something that happens because a person let their guard down or simply wasn't thinking clearly.

So how do you shield your heart and forgive at the same

time? I call it all-inclusive forgiveness. This not only absolves the offender of the wrong, but relieves them of your desire to condemn or inflict punishment because of the wrong. There are no strings attached—no ifs, ands, or buts—just an acknowledgment that the error has been erased. This is what complete forgiveness looks like.

This, however, does not mean that your heart will not be broken, or you will not feel pain or lose trust. The healing of the hurt and the forgiving of the wrong seldom happen at the same time. Forgiveness can be complete even though the healing is not. If you truly love someone, you cannot shield your heart from pain. The risk of loving brings with it the risk of being hurt. You can't avoid that. And the object of forgiveness is not to shield your heart from the hurt, but to strengthen and mature it through the power of pardon.

For too long I've seen couples struggle with what it actually means to forgive. They let fear prevent them from experiencing the emotional catharsis that comes with releasing their partner from judgment for the wrongs they've committed. In my estimation, this kind of cleansing is the only way you can move forward after a serious issue has confronted the relationship.

Forgiveness should bring with it a great deal of emotional freedom. You should feel as if you just relieved yourself of a heaviness that has been weighing you down. So if you claim to forgive and you still feel this burden, you have not truly absolved your partner of the offense and you haven't freed yourself of the feelings of failure or inadequacy that often accompany a major challenge.

There is an often-repeated quote from the English poet Alexander Pope that I like. In the poem *An Essay on Criticism*, written in 1709, he gives his take on the human condition in regard to forgiveness:

Ah ne'er so dire a thirst of glory boast,
Nor in the critic let the man be lost!
Good nature and good sense must ever join;
To err is human; to forgive, divine.

(Part II, lines 522–25)

In his old-fashioned poetic English, Pope basically says not to allow pride to overcome you as it does with critical people who are lost in their own boasting. Allow good judgment and a good heart to prevail. Everyone does bad things every now and then, but to forgive is an act from heaven.

The last line is the most familiar to us: *To err is human; to forgive, divine.* Already we can see that forgiveness is not something that's easy for us mere mortals. To allow someone who has truly hurt you to stay in your life and to experience love from you as though they never hurt you seems absolutely crazy. But anything short of total absolution is not complete forgiveness.

To fully comprehend the depth of all-inclusive forgiveness, allow me to look at how Christianity views forgiveness. As a student of religion and somewhat of a theologian, I have found this explanation is one that can be used irrespective of a person's spiritual or religious background. Moreover, almost every religion or belief system teaches the power of complete forgiveness in some form.

The entire purpose of Jesus the Messiah was to show His great love for humanity through His persecution and death on a cross at a Roman execution. Since He was the Messiah, His physical death constituted a spiritual pardon for all the sins of humanity. It denoted an absolution of sins committed in the past, in the present, and any future sins. It is all-inclusive. The only action required of the wrongdoer is to accept this forgiveness. The doctrine teaches that there is nothing that makes a person worthy of it. It is given by grace out of God's pure love for humankind.

This is how I understand forgiveness. It is a complete abandoning of judgment and resentment for the person who has wronged you. It is a pardon of what the offender did, what he or she is doing, and also forgiving the possibility that it may happen again.

This is not a popular view. Often when we forgive, we have strings attached. The attitude is, *I'll forgive you, but if you ever do it again…* This is an absolutely reasonable way to think. Why would you dare expose yourself to any future pain without some assurances? But there is one thing you must understand. If your forgiveness has that caveat attached to it, you will continually be on the lookout to see if that condition has been breached.

I have talked to numerous hurt people who claim to forgive their partner, yet still search through their phones constantly. They stand watch to make sure their spouse is toeing the line and not making the same mistake again as a way of protecting themselves from future hurt. This kind of constant supervision and surveillance places both parties in an emotional prison. It doesn't feel like forgiveness because it's not.

My wife and I were in a conversation with a struggling couple. The wife defiantly declared that she had forgiven her husband, but she was still punishing him. She was often angry and treated him disrespectfully. While we understood this was all coming from a place of pain, the fact remains that if you truly forgive someone, you actually release them from your retribution.

True forgiveness not only forgives the act a person has committed, but also forgives the actor. It is a far-reaching umbrella that covers the entire person. It does not concern itself with whether a person will mess up again because it is not act based; it is condition based. You are forgiving the person's condition, not just what they did. This is why Alexander Pope referred to it as divine. Anything less is incomplete and falls woefully short of true forgiveness.

In order for that kind of forgiveness to occur, someone has to be the neutralizing agent toward all the bad feelings and all the wrong that has entered the marriage from the negative event. It cannot be a situation where both parties are experiencing painful emotions constantly. There cannot be resolution when both persons are experiencing emotional trauma. Someone has to be the healing agent, the remedy for the relationship. Forgiveness contains the ingredients for that remedy.

All this being said, there is a notion that when a person forgives, they are supposed to forget. This is utter nonsense. As humans, we learn from our past experiences. We know not to touch a hot stove because we tried it once before—and once was enough. Our life experiences teach us how to order ourselves and how to initiate boundaries, so we don't have to go through those negative events again.

When a person is wronged, it is a lesson learned. The exoneration of that wrong is a completely different issue from the experience you've gained out of that challenge. While the lesson helps you set future boundaries, the forgiveness frees you of carrying the weight of that issue. Forgiveness is ultimately meant to benefit the person who was injured. Its whole purpose is to release you from worry, stress, and frustration.

Now, here's the tough part: If you choose to forgive, and forgive all-inclusively, can you live with the fact that it may happen again? Are your love and desire for your mate strong enough for you to stay, knowing that there is a possibility that it could happen again?

I have counseled couples who have chosen to stay and forgive. They have to take on a new mindset. They have to see the issue as a challenge that they both are fighting even though only one is actually perpetrating the deed.

This happens when a spouse is addicted to a substance and may have caused great harm to the family. Choosing to stay and forgive means you will see them through to recovery. It means the struggling spouse will not feel your judgment, but your love. They will feel your forgiveness, and it is that which often serves as an impetus for them to recover.

The same is true of an adulterous relationship or of any other issue that may not be as major. If a person chooses to stay, they must understand that the struggle has just begun. They must have the mental, emotional, and spiritual fortitude to see their spouse as damaged and seeking healing. The fact that you have released your resentment because you've chosen to forgive will assist you in focusing on the problem instead of the person.

This is not an easy thing to do. It takes reaching deep within your soul to find out what about the issue hurts you so badly. You must spend time in meditation or prayer so you can find your center and not be controlled by your emotions. This is a time to take control of how you feel and not let your moods run rampant.

Capture every negative thought, bring it to light, and compare it with reason. Then decide how you're going to proceed.

This is what forgiveness looks like.

Now, of course, as I tell couples in these circumstances, you do have options. You can forgive and stay or you can forgive and leave. But you must forgive. Even if you choose to leave, which we will cover more in chapter 14, the fact is that you must leave without resentment. You must completely resolve the issues in your heart and make it known to your spouse that you have, in fact, forgiven them.

Forgiving this way actually infuses you with power. It raises you to a place where you are not a victim or weak. Weaklings don't have the power to forgive in this manner. It takes fortitude and maturity to be able to look at someone who hurt you badly and then look at your own failings and conclude that because you've been forgiven in your past, you are compelled to be just as honorable. You are grateful enough and self-assured enough to release someone from their misdeeds because you can consider that you would want the same grace to be shown if it were you.

CHAPTER 12

Punks Don't Make Love— They Screw

Gerry and Sasha had known each other since high school. They always liked each other, but he was a confirmed Casanova and she had always been a good girl—the kind all the guys wanted but no one could get. Now as adults, the game had completely changed.

Gerry happened to see Sasha a few years after college graduation and was overtaken by the beautiful woman she had grown into. She was impressed that he had quit breaking hearts. They dated, and the high school spark reignited. Nearly a year later, they were married.

The wedding was small but beautiful. After their honeymoon on a lush tropical island, they returned home and moved in together. This was a fairy-tale life. He was a banker and she was a dentist. Now it was time for real life. They resumed their jobs and everyday lives and had an active and fulfilling sex life—at least for her.

A few months after living the dream, Gerry decided to call me. After some pleasantries, he said, "Marriage is no joke, is it? I'm struggling with something, man!"

I listened quietly as he continued, "You mean I have to have sex with this one woman for the rest of my life? I don't think I can do it!"

Sadly, Gerry's words were prophetic. After about ten months of marriage, he had numerous affairs.

My counsel to this wayward husband was simple and effective, had he chosen to listen. I told him, "The problem is that you didn't stop screwing your spouse." When you marry, the intimate relationship you have with your mate should elevate beyond the mere physical act of adolescent intercourse and enter into the realm of loving, intimate interchange.

Interchange is an emotional state where a person not only is concerned about getting personal, visceral satisfaction, but is making love the way their partner wants to receive love. Imagine if your partner was making love to you as though you were them. This is the idea of sexual interchange. It's a complete immersion into each other, through knowing and implementing what the other person desires emotionally and physically. Interchange is where screwing ends and lovemaking begins.

CREATING ATTRACTION

Let's look at what "intercourse" actually is. It literally means communication or dealings between two people. It's transactional in nature; a simple connecting or dealing with another party. This is a description of sexual relations at their minimum level.

However, the higher plane of lovemaking exists at the

interchange of emotions. So having intercourse will provide the enjoyable act of sex. But having interchange brings the passion, understanding, and mutual creativity of lovemaking. This is where couples are actually looking at love through the other person's eyes and perspectives. Hence, it requires a great deal of communication to reach that goal.

I have discovered that in nearly all the couples my wife and I have coached, even the ones with sexual infrequency, they seldom ask about what things to do in the bedroom. Usually they want to discuss other issues. They want to communicate better or want to open up and become vulnerable. In most cases, when these goals are achieved, the act of sex takes care of itself.

That being said, one question couples do ask is about their attraction for their mate. "How do I develop desire or create romance in my marriage?" The answer is simple: by creating attraction. No, that is not sarcasm. Attraction is created by simply doing the things you do when you are attracted.

A great number of people feel that attraction is a thing that floats around out there and either you have it or you don't. If you're fortunate, you will find it and then that elusive thing called *chemistry* will be there. Now, I have no idea who postulated the idea of chemistry when it comes to attraction, but I take issue with it. While I do believe there is a certain biological chemistry that happens when people are attracted to each other, it is not random.

Think back to high school science class. Most of us have had the experience of making chemical reactions happen. If you combine baking soda and vinegar, there will be a volcanic foaming reaction. It is something that you actively do to create a reaction.

Attraction is the same. All chemistry can be created. To create something is to bring it into existence when it didn't previously exist. It's akin to making something appear when everything inside is telling you it can't be there or it can't exist. The first step is to do things that you would do as though you *were* attracted. Acting as though you were attracted will eventually lead you to feeling attracted.

This sounds simple, and to some it may seem disingenuous—as though you are forcing something. But that is not the case. You must learn to create chemistry in your relationship irrespective of attraction because there will come a point when age and time will diminish beauty. When it does, it will behoove you to have learned that attraction is more than just some ethereal presence hovering around a person.

I've always believed beauty is just a résumé. It only gets you a seat at the table. After you are in the conversation, you must bring something substantial or know how to create it. This is a vital point.

In a marriage, you will do the things to create attraction or chemistry only if you are committed to making your relationship better. While most people seeking attraction in relationships are depending on feelings to occur, sometimes what it takes is just plain effort. It is a matter of doing what you may not feel at the time, with the expectation that the feelings will come. To create passion in marriage, you must make feelings and attraction follow your actions as opposed to letting feelings lead.

THREE TYPES OF LOVERS

When discussing sex with couples, I've found there are three types of lovers. I use the word "lovers" loosely, because I don't want to confuse having sex with being in love. Simply put, you can have sex without being in love, but it's difficult to be in love without having sex. However, for these purposes, we're referring to couples in a committed love relationship.

The Hunter

The first type of lover is the *hunter*. Those who go after sex and intimacy at any cost. A hunter may be male or female. There is no preferred time or place for sex, and they make it known. They don't seem to have any problem initiating or going after what they want.

Hunters may not care if they are physically attracted or if their spouse's body has changed or isn't what it used to be. It's not so much about physical attraction as much as physical satisfaction. They go for what they want and initiate without hesitation.

This is how Gerry was as a single man. He took initiative and was confident enough to make his intentions clear and unquestionable. His voracious sexual appetite, however, could not be contained, which led to his marital problems and subsequent divorce.

On the positive side, hunters always make their partners feel wanted and desired. After all, who doesn't want to be pursued? These are the couples where either the husband or the wife is constantly flirting and showing public displays of affection. They may go for only short times without touching each other.

The hunter's boldness and adventurous attitude keep excitement in the marriage. Even if the couple is one-sided when it comes to initiating sex, that's okay. The hunter is fine with being the one who initiates because they are getting what they want. In fact, I know couples where one spouse initiates intimacy the great majority of the time and they both are fine with it. In this type of relationship, when the hunter can stay committed, both parties can have a long-lasting sex life with their mate.

The Target

The second type of lover is the *target*. These are the people who wait for love or sex to find them. I've found that most people live in this space, since most people are afraid to be hurt. Consequently, they want to make sure their lover wants them first before they reveal their desire.

If both parties in the relationship are targets, there may be long periods of sexual drought. This is not because there is no desire for intimacy, but rather both parties are afraid to initiate and are waiting to be wanted. Unless someone adopts the hunter attitude, they both will be sexually frustrated.

Targets want to feel wanted and desired and will look at their spouse's lack of initiation as a sign that their spouse actually does not love them. This may not be the case in the slightest bit. They may simply be married to another target. They both are waiting for some kind of advance and no one is communicating it. So they both feel unwanted and unloved.

When a target is finally sexually approached, it creates a sense of security. They feel they are loved and will give themselves totally to their partner. They tend to judge their sexual worth based on whether their mate approaches them, but if they want a completely fulfilling experience, they need to come out of their safety zone and approach their spouse.

Equal Opportunity

The third type is the equal opportunity (EO) lover. These people tend to have an equal approach to love and have developed a certain style of give and take. If they see what they want, they pursue it. If they want to be pursued, they'll wait, but not to their own detriment.

The EO lover usually has a comfortable self-image and has a greater sexual maturity. They are not frustrated if sex has a short drought and are not intimidated if there are times of plenty. They simply go with the flow. When both parties have this attitude, they don't care who initiates sex in the marriage, as long as they are both satisfied with the results.

MARS AND VENUS

I need to discuss male and female attitudes as far as sex is concerned. There are so many different philosophies about how men and women think about this topic. While some of them are true, much is conjecture. There is a large body of research from great minds who have studied and written on this topic ad nauseum. I will not reiterate their hypotheses, but here's a general understanding.

First, although this is not true in every case, men generally tend to be more goal focused in regard to sex—and the goal is to reach climax. This is neither good nor bad, unless he's the only one reaching the goal. It's just the way it is and the sensitive man will want to creatively include his wife. How the couple does that has to be discussed.

Men tend to be externally driven. They are more excited by what they see. Feelings can catch up later, but the physical tends to hold more value. Men are attracted to the physical before they can even get to know the emotional, more lasting side of their mate. Even though it may seem like men are still living in the Neanderthal era, their primary desire for physical attraction should not be criticized, but rather understood.

Lastly, men tend to be service oriented. After a man has been intimate with his spouse, he may want to know whether the goal was achieved. Performance is the measuring tool. Emotion is the result.

Next, let's look at what happens when a woman wants to make love to her husband. Again, this may not be true in every case, but she tends to be more process focused. Climax is an event in the process but not the entire goal. Although women do want to experience it, both the process and the goal are important to them.

Women tend to be internally, not externally, driven. Her heart and emotions will drive her actions. She wants to know whether there are feelings involved and whether there is respect and value during the process. The physicality can catch up later.

Women are also quality oriented over quantity. With most women, sex is not a race or a competition. They are not trying to see if they can get the job done. Again, this is neither a bad nor a good thing; it just is. Emotions are the measuring tool. Performance is the result.

In a perfect world, women and men should complement and balance each other in regard to sex. There should be a give-and-take and a shared experience where, although both genders are different and think and behave in different ways, those differences are compatible.

Honestly, I have not dedicated a great deal of this book to the act of sex. That's because I believe sex is the result of a great relationship where all the positively functioning elements are present. I have yet to see a couple who is communicating deeply and effectively, sharing vulnerably, respecting each other, and productively arguing—and are still having sex issues.

Great sex is the outgrowth of a successful relationship and is completely subjective to the parties participating in it. I believe it's all about communication; the greater you communicate, the more you will want to be close. Ultimately, this closeness will culminate in sexual intimacy because loving sex is the highest and most intimate form of positive communication between couples. This is where sexual interchange happens; when a couple has emotionally and verbally shared to the point where the act is not even the goal. The goal is lost in becoming intimately, emotionally, and physically one with each other.

Ultimately, what goes on in the bedroom is an exact reflection of what goes on before you get to the bedroom. The most powerful sex organ is the brain. Whatever a person constantly thinks about and talks about is what they will live out in their lives. The intimacy of a couple's conversation is a telltale sign of whether they are having a satisfying sex life. When tension is removed and emotional walls come down and you like each other and enjoy talking, sex will be inevitable, and it will be great.

AFFAIRS IN THE HEAD VS. AFFAIRS IN THE BED

Gerry and Sasha never had a fair chance to make their marriage work. Gerry never really emotionally settled into the marriage. He thought legally binding himself to his new wife would cure him of his insatiable sexual hunger, but it didn't.

Even though he managed to stay monogamous during their courtship and engagement, Sasha often caught his eyes wandering. A few times he answered texts from questionable women from his past but managed to keep them at bay. When Sasha caught Gerry looking at suspicious websites, he just brushed it off as male curiosity.

But it wasn't just curiosity at all. Gerry had not cut ties with his past. He was not finished with his previous life of one-night stands and meeting women at bars. And though he may not have gone bar hopping during their marriage, he was living there in his mind.

He found himself constantly measuring his wife against the paramours of his past. In such a state, he could never be satisfied with his wife. He was still having affairs in the head. He was living out his previous fantasies while with his wife. They were his motivation for arousal.

It wasn't long before the affairs in the head became affairs in the bed, which should be no surprise. It is virtually impossible to separate your intimate thoughts from your actions. All actions begin with conception. They begin in the mind and then are acted out in reality.

For that reason, most affairs happen long before the sexual act takes place. In most cases, the groundwork has been set with casual flirting or supposedly harmless interactions. Relationships are vulnerable. Even the best ones are not foolproof against intruders. Safeguards must be taken to gird up the walls of your relationships so that no breaches in the fortress are noticed by those who want to get your attention.

To safely protect your marriage against affairs, you must be aware of the gateways to affairs. Let's consider some of the areas that can lead to affairs in the bed.

SEXUAL FANTASIES

Sexual fantasy is often used as a way of keeping or creating spice in a marriage. But this can easily lead to unwanted trouble. Sexual fantasies create unrealistic expectations for your spouse. To dream about the astonishing exploits of imaginary people can create standards that no one can live up to.

Sometimes when a person fantasizes about others as foreplay, it becomes an issue of transference. Meaning, a spouse is attempting to play out the fantasy of being intimate with someone else. Those thoughts have a tendency to run wild if not checked. Seldom is anyone comfortable with being compared to a fantasy. It makes them feel they can't measure up, or that their mate prefers the fantasy over them.

With this being said, I've spoken to a number of couples who feel sexual fantasies are perfectly acceptable as long as they are kept in the head and not revealed. This may sound good, but what such people don't understand is that fantasies can grow leaps and bounds beyond what reality can do. There are no limits to what you can imagine. And as willing as your spouse may be, it's nearly impossible to keep up with satisfying your unrestricted whims— which often leads to searching for someone who can.

PORNOGRAPHY

Pornography can be another gateway to an affair. I am a firm believer in letting people determine the rules of their own bedroom. No one has a right to dictate the intimacy rules between a husband and a wife. However, those rules must be agreed upon and they must never create unfair or impossible comparisons. When they do, the inequity can tear at the fabric of a couple's trust and intimacy.

Actors are paid to be great. To portray something that appeases your wildest dreams. All movies are only portraying characters, and seldom can "regular" people imitate those roles. In terms of pornography, no average human can perform the exploits of these paid actors. Nor should they be forced to. Again, this is creating unfair expectations that few spouses can live up to.

Some may dismiss porn as merely a way to get in the mood. But when other exciting and erotic images are placed into your mind, your brain may not be able to distinguish between fantasy and reality. This is why there is a physical reaction to the visual presentation. It's impossible to compete with experienced acting and Photoshop.

FLIRTING

"Harmless" flirting is another gateway to an affair. Whether or not you find another person sexually attractive, sex can happen when you are not expecting it. There is a purely biological and instinctive component to the sex act. Animals have sex because of instinct or heat. Humans can have that same tendency. What separates us from animals is the ethical and/or spiritual imperative that guides us.

Flirting is an example of presenting the dessert, smelling it, and describing it—yet without ever eating it. After being in executive sales for over a decade, I found that flirting is a big part of sales. People can get the product anywhere. What they buy is the salesperson. Often flirtatious selling is what gets the job done.

But in a business setting, boundaries must be constantly observed. I saw many instances, when I was a single and free corporate salesperson, where the lines could have been easily blurred. The act of complimenting and being friendly in order to reach a sales goal can easily be twisted into something more salacious. For me, it was necessary to have a business-only goal in mind and to clearly make known to my client what that goal was. Most of the time a person will not cross that line, unless there is a clear invitation to do so.

However, when the goal is not defined and an invitation is presented, it becomes sexual flirting. In this case, the whole goal is to put the other person at ease and lure them in so that an intimate opportunity can be made available. Needless to say, many have crashed and burned by not being disciplined enough to know the difference.

EMOTIONAL INTIMACY

Emotional sharing is yet another opening to an illicit relationship. There should be an impenetrable bond between husband and wife. For this reason, it is never wise to share sexual or any other intimate information with anyone who is not your spouse.

The familiarity of this kind of communication brings you into another person's emotional space. Such deep trust will typically crave closer contact. It will beg for more emotional interaction. Most couples I've counseled who have had affairs agree that it began with emotional sharing. Their initial intentions were pure. They simply needed someone to listen. But listening led to attraction. Attraction led to touching. And touching led to intimacy.

Don't deceive yourself. Most people can tell when they are getting too close to the fire. Your spouse can see it as well. Honesty and self-evaluation are mandatory so that you will always understand your limits.

The best safeguard against affairs is the ability to communicate needs and desires. If something is missing in the marriage, revealing the absence of that thing and then discussing how it can be retrieved are the key to avoiding impropriety. I've found that a number of couples don't communicate deeply enough to discover genuine intimate needs and desires. To actually talk about fantasies, whether they're possible or not, is a necessity in a healthy relationship.

TALK ABOUT IT

There are three levels of communication I want to stress at this point that will go a long way to safeguarding your marriage. Since sexual intimacy is the deepest form of communication, it's necessary for a couple to scale beyond the superficial levels of interaction. Being at this level with your spouse should remove the need to experience intimacy outside of your marriage.

The first level is reserved for people who don't have deep connections. Level One communication is normally about events and facts. It's usually composed of closed questions such as: "How's the weather?" "What happened at work today?" "What's for dinner?"

Couples default to this level of conversation when there is an unresolved issue in the relationship. It's as though they revert back to when they first met in order to protect themselves. Such a conversational reversion can also lead to avoiding physical contact. A couple may be comfy and snuggle every night, but at this level, they sleep on opposite sides of the bed.

Or a husband may be accustomed to opening the door for his wife whenever they go out. However, when the communication reverts back to the primary level, she is quick to open the door for herself or he will avoid it. Any kind of intimate kindness is avoided and partners go back to what I refer to as the *first-date phase*.

Needless to say, when either person reverts back to this level, intimacy or sex is often out of the question. If there is no deep communication, there will be no deep intimacy. This is because there is an incontrovertible link between intimacy and communication.

The second level phase of interaction usually focuses on ideas and opinions. This includes open questions such as: "What do you think about the kids' grades?" "What is your opinion on getting another house?" "Do you love me?"

I have found the majority of marriages exist at this Level Two stage of conversation. This is the *third-date phase*. You are not willing to divulge everything about yourself, but you definitely have an interest and want to know more.

There is minor or coincidental physical contact at this stage. This might lead to comfortable but not close intimacy. In some cases there may be sex, but not usually, and it's easy to delay it, since you don't feel that close yet.

It's at this stage where marriages fall into the average category.

It's at the third level of communication, which I call the

engagement phase, that couples lose inhibitions and want to be as close as they possibly can. This is the ideal space a couple wants to live in. This is where they honestly discuss feelings, emotions, hopes, and dreams and include each other in their plans. They buy into one another's dreams and want to accomplish everything together.

When a married couple is at this level of interchange, sex is not an issue or even a conversation. It's a natural part of the relationship and no one feels neglected. Because of their mutual trust, they are willing to discuss any emotions without the fear of being criticized or judged. Level Three communication is characterized by open and deep questions such as: "What can I do to make you happy?" "How do you feel about where we are in our marriage?" "How do you know you love me?"

Sex is a natural part of the marriage. Few marriages can survive without it. But sex must evolve when placed inside the marriage union. The adolescent screwing that takes place when you're single is supposed to conclude, and a nobler, more elevated idea of physical and emotional intimacy should emerge.

Intercourse is elevated to sexual interchange. Deeper and more substantive communication creates a place where sexual intimacy is not something to be worked on, but rather something that has grown out of an impenetrable union between two mutually vulnerable people. You're not waiting for chemistry to happen, but you both create it by constantly discovering the wonder and value that exists in each other.

Wandering eyes and desires to find intimacy outside the relationship are not an option because you realize what the two of you have built together and you're unwilling to let anything or anyone come between your treasured union. When a couple can get to this point, they have built an emotional fortress around their relationship that will not allow others to enter. They have closed the gateways to illicit associations.

This is what sex in marriage should look like. This is how it's intended to be. And this is what's possible when two people intentionally do the work to make it so.

CHAPTER 13

Punks Just Want to Be Happy

Tonya picked up her cup of coffee from the counter in the home of her mom, Sarah. They both walked over to the dining table to sit down for a chat. Sarah reached over and lovingly placed her hand over her daughter's. They were accustomed to coming together to share heartfelt issues.

"Do you feel you are ready to take this next step, honey?" Sarah asked. "I mean, are you sure this is what you really want?"

Tonya leaned back in her seat to gather her thoughts. She knew her mom had invited her there to find out more about her relationship with Chad, her boyfriend. Chad and Tonya met online and things seemed to take off from there. He dropped out of college to start a graphic design business with his buddies. The pay was slow but steady. Tonya had graduated from college and was now working as a customer service rep at a bank.

They had dated for three months before moving in together, a decision her parents were not very fond of. They had raised Tonya to wait until marriage before having sex, much less moving in with someone. Regardless of their objection to her living situation, they were still supportive of their daughter and wanted the best for her—that is, until Tonya told them she and Chad were planning to be married in a few months.

Sarah sat there waiting for a response to her question. "Honey? Do you really know what you want? What marriage is all about?"

Tonya leaned forward and grabbed her mom's hand with both of hers. She smiled as though she were entertaining a fond memory of Chad, then she calmly and confidently stated, "He makes me happy, Mom. We make each other happy."

Sarah's smile began to crack, as though her assumptions about her daughter's unreadiness to marry had just been proven. She looked at her daughter sympathetically and then lovingly replied, "Sweetie, that's lovely, but happiness is not the goal of marriage."

A LOUSY GOAL

For all the people I have encountered who are longing to be married and build a family, they will often talk about their goal of being happy. They romanticize marriage to the point where they believe it will be a fantasy. And while that feeling is admirable, if they expect marriage to last for the long haul, they have to consider what it looks like once the feelings subside.

In nearly three decades of performing weddings, I have stood in front of countless adorable couples and had them recite their vows: "To have and to hold, for better or worse, for richer or poorer, in sickness and in health and forsaking all others, 'til death do us part."

No other words can increase heartbeats and cause sweats as

much as these. Impeccably dressed, innocent, expectant couples with visions of sugary sweet marriages dancing through their minds drink up the sentiments expressed in those vows and expect only the best. They see themselves dancing and cavorting hand in hand, ready to change the entire world. This will be the love story to end all love stories, they dream.

And some of them are absolutely right. Some have amazing love stories and feel, years later, that marriage has been an answer to their sincerest prayers.

But there are others who soon find that the bunny rabbits in their dreams are actually carnivorous, bloodthirsty beasts who devour their souls, and that the rainbows are monochromatic clouds that only cast dark shadows over their lives.

Even so, these two categories of couples are as much alike as they are different. They both begin with the best of intentions: They want to be happy.

One question I often ask couples after their marital bliss has subsided is, *What is the goal of your marriage?* Normally, this question is followed by moments of mutual silence. Then the couple slowly turns toward each other with quizzical expressions, hoping the other person will answer.

Whether newlyweds or marriage veterans, very few couples consider the goal of their marriage. Sadly, most of the couples I've encountered basically just want to be happy. Happiness becomes the *thing* they spend their matrimonial lives trying to acquire. Everything they do as a couple is judged by whether or not they are happy when doing it or at least as a result of it.

Let me offer the straightforward truth: Making happiness the goal of marriage is one of the most serious mistakes a couple can make.

Don't get me wrong. I understand the goal of being happy.

> Let me offer the straightforward truth: Making happiness the goal of marriage is one of the most serious mistakes a couple can make.

Who doesn't want it? Who doesn't want to always look at their partner with eyes of intense desire and just want to consume them each moment of the day? Who wouldn't want to experience the euphoric explosions that occur in the pit of the stomach when things are going well?

But in order for me to fully understand anything, I must be able to describe it. So what does happiness look like? Can you touch it or taste it? Oh yes, you can definitely feel it, but can you control it? Can you intentionally achieve it?

There must be something deeper—something much more substantial—in a marriage goal than just elation.

KNOW WHERE YOU'RE GOING

Most couples I've encountered have never really considered what happiness (or even love for that matter) looks like. So let's establish some principles together.

First of all, happiness can never be the goal of a marriage. It can never be the end game for two people pledging their lives to each other. That is not to say happiness isn't important in a marriage, but it must not be the end result. There is no place called *happy* in a marriage, where once you've gotten there, all is well and you both are successful.

Why? Because happiness is always the outcome of an enjoyable pursuit or thing. It is the by-product of something that has been accomplished. Hence, people are happy because of many different things.

There are some things other people do that seem incredibly uninteresting to me. Bird-watching, fishing, and collecting pretty much anything (except cars) are just a few of the things that don't hold any happiness for me. Yet there are people who dedicate their lives to these pastimes. They make them happy. Happiness is completely relative. We all may have different things or different nuances of things that bring us joy.

That being said, how can two people even know when they have reached a place where they are both experiencing the same glee in their relationship? Because, inevitably, spouses will have different things that make them happy.

My wife and I certainly have different things that make us happy. One thing she enjoys is shopping; just to look at things and compare. She may or may not buy anything. It can be online or at a shopping center. It makes no difference because the joy is in the actual event. This is beyond my comprehension. When I reluctantly go with her to a store, the great majority of the time I'm only smiling on the outside, while my insides are being eaten alive by boredom. Even if I have to shop for myself, I do it as if I have a mission to accomplish. I know what I want. I secure the target, and I strike as quickly and as efficiently as possible. Mission accomplished!

I, on the other hand, love to take a break and watch a good movie—something brainless where I don't have to think. It's my getaway. I'll sometimes sit with Wendy and we'll watch something that I'm really into, and I see her sitting there facing the television but she's shopping on her phone.

It's perfectly okay to have different interests and different objects of joy, but the point is that it's barely possible to have a mutual goal with a thing that is so relative as happiness. Someone will always be not as happy as the other. There must be something more substantive that becomes the goal of the marriage.

That's the second principle. The goal for your marriage must be something substantive that both spouses mutually agree to set for the relationship.

Unfortunately, this is something few couples do prior to marrying. While it's customary to do this for a career path, an education, or even a competitive sport, when it comes to marriage, people often just have the ceremony and expect the best without setting any goals to accomplish.

The most successful marriages know where they're going. They understand that their relationship is an opportunity to accomplish something great. They are legally bound together for a specific purpose. It may be something different from any other relationship you know of, but it's something the two of you understand, and it's something achievable.

When Wendy and I were married, we both understood the lessons we had learned from our pasts. We mutually decided that our *marriage goal* would be to help couples avoid the same pitfalls we experienced in our previously failed marriages. It was important that we achieve something lasting that was important to us. Out of this desire, our marriage organization was born.

Marriage goals will be different for each couple. Both must clearly understand what they as a team can reasonably accomplish. This is highly personal and should be talked about consciously.

Ideally, this should take place before a couple decides to tie the knot. They should write their marriage plan. Meaning, they should organize and determine what they plan to accomplish in the marriage. Go into it with direction. Make adjustments along the way, because as you both grow, your objectives may shift. This will require a revisiting of the goals and maybe restructuring. I've seen couples do this yearly or as needed.

I know some may think that this takes the romance and adventure out of marriage. On the contrary, the adventure comes in dodging the roadblocks and toppling the blockades together on your journey. The romance will come in the fact that the two of you are learning about each other's strengths and challenges. You are communicating and planning. You are a team.

Then, with each accomplishment along the way, you will experience happiness. There is nothing more joyful that watching a plan come to fruition. If you've planned on having children, then knowing this is something you both want and seeing the outcome is exhilarating. Or if your goal is to establish a business and change a particular industry, the accomplishment again brings the happiness. But there must be a goal or goals in order to make it happen.

The consequences of each milestone you reach will be a growing respect and mutual admiration. There will be a feeling of pleasure that you've done it together. These are the basics of building a life together, as opposed to expecting happiness to just happen.

There are many couples I've counseled who express their frustration at not having joy in their relationship, while finding great fulfillment in other areas of their lives. For example, there are people who are very successful and happy at their jobs, and yet unsuccessful and unhappy in their relationships. I believe that's because some don't see the two as having equal value.

At work, people have incentives. They want to be self-actualized by being promoted and being congratulated by their coworkers. They want their name on the door or that corner office. They get a rush out of being seen and known as successful. There is also the paycheck, which to many is a direct reflection of their value.

In relationships, people don't have the same drive or the same goals. They may not look at their relationship as benefiting them in the same manner. They may not get that high from marriage accomplishments.

The motivators in your marriage should be greater than those in your career. There should be greater value and greater happiness. No one should feel better going to work than they do coming home. People are motivated to go to work because of camaraderie, the feeling of accomplishment, but mostly because of the paycheck and what it can buy for them and their family.

Your career should be your lesser mode of happiness. Home and family should always bring greater lasting joy. At home you should be motivated by creating a family legacy from a family business. Or maybe building lasting traditions centered around holidays or signal events in the family could be an inspiration, or focusing on the children's accomplishments and guiding them to success. In the years to come, children remember family accomplishments and love shared much more than they'll remember Dad's promotion or Mom's executive corner office.

Your relationship has to be bigger than the two of you. It has to have loftier goals than just being a source of temporary good feelings. The feelings of happiness are created as a result of the actions you've taken to secure a positive future. It is not a haphazard explosion of emotions, but rather the outcome of calculated decisions.

Many expect happiness to come and get them as though it's just *out there* waiting. They expect it to waft in on waves of serenity and overtake them. Happiness doesn't come that way. It doesn't search for people; it exists for everyone at the crossroads of effort and preparation.

CHAPTER 14

When Punking Out Is Necessary

Sarah approached me one day on the campus where I was an adjunct professor; a deathly serious look on her face. She was a professional colleague and a longtime friend, so I knew that look. Besides, I had seen it on individuals' faces many times before as they sat for couple's counseling. Sarah was having marital trouble and she needed help immediately.

As we talked, I found out that her husband, Levi, had been cheating on her and had been caught red-handed. He was a decent husband otherwise but could not seem to stop sleeping around. This was the second time she'd caught him, so he wasn't very good at cheating.

Sarah sat me down and, with a somber look of defeat, asked me, "Should I leave him? I'm so tired of living like this! He has cheated twice that I know of, and I just don't think I can do this any longer."

I asked, "Why are you asking what I think?"

"Because I want to be sure," she responded.

"And what I say to you will make you sure? Don't you already *know* what you should do?" I replied. "Do you really need my opinion?"

She said, "I guess not, but I'm just so confused."

I told her I wanted to ask some questions, starting with, "Do you love him?"

Without hesitation, she answered, "Yes!"

"Is he a benefit or detriment to you and the kids?"

She thought for a moment, then said, "As long as the kids are not affected by his foolishness, he's a real benefit."

"If you stay, will he be willing to get therapy?"

She replied, "He said he would."

Then I asked, "If you leave, will you miss him and will you feel as though you should have fought for your marriage?"

She said, "Probably so . . . yes."

The conclusion was obvious. She stayed, and they did get counseling. For a while, Levi tried to change his behavior. He was the model husband for a time, and with counseling he endeavored to change the way he viewed his marriage. His counselor was able to help him discover the roots of his destructive behavior, and he realized he wanted his family.

Unfortunately, the woman he'd had the earlier affair with wasn't finished with their relationship. Within six months after starting therapy, Levi and Sarah were notified that the woman was pregnant. Levi found out that sometimes a careless action like an affair can yield lifelong results.

For Sarah, the idea that she would have to be connected to this woman and the new baby for life was too much. So she decided to end the marriage.

Sarah had been willing and ready to fight for her marriage. She had forgiven Levi for his previous unfaithfulness and wanted to push through and make it work. But now their children were aware of the infidelity, and they were starting to be affected. They saw their mom crying uncontrollably at night after arguing about the affair, and they were starting to resent their dad.

The house had become an unhealthy environment whenever Levi was around. Plus, he was adamant about not severing the relationship with his new child and the mother. In fact, he wanted Sarah and the kids to understand that his attention and parenting would be divided now. This was more than any of them could take.

THE RIGHT TIME TO LEAVE

Sometimes it's not being a punk if you decide to leave a marriage. I have talked to more than a few couples who have been confronted with whether they should end their marriage. Probably contrary to what a traditional pastor would say, I don't tell them all to stay under any circumstances. In fact, I've suggested to quite a few that remaining in their marriage would be harmful if things didn't drastically change.

So when do you know it's the right time to call it quits? Let me first say that I've seen couples recover from almost anything you can imagine. I've personally known and counseled marriages that have risen from the ashes after acts of violence, infidelity, addiction, financial ruin, and so much more.

But there is no case where I would encourage a person to stay if they are either in danger or putting someone else in danger. Of course, each couple has to make their own decision in that regard. These grave marital decisions cannot be coerced, because only those involved in the marriage have to live with the consequences.

Just as it takes two people to successfully contribute to a thriving marriage, it also takes both parties, giving conscious effort, to map a proper exit. Even when one spouse is not cooperating and seems to want to cause discord, there must at least be civility on one side in order to advance the process.

Here's my opinion: The right time to leave a marriage is whenever a person has determined that staying will cause them irreparable harm. I say irreparable because there is always some harm caused in even great marriages. But most marital injury can be healed or, at the very least, endured until time has had the chance to deaden the pain.

However, there are those times when the risk of staying far outweighs the benefits. In such cases, it would be irresponsible to yourself and your family to continue in something that could cause far-reaching damage. Separating yourself may be the only option.

Still, there is a right way to accomplish such a separation.

THE RIGHT WAY TO LEAVE

I'm always saddened when marriages break up because I've seen so many people feel as though they are failures as a result. Irrespective of whose fault it was, spouses often believe there was something they could have done. Or they feel there was something they didn't do that could have made a difference.

However, a failed marriage does not make a failed person. It is not always an indictment of a person's character,

> **A failed marriage does not make a failed person.**

and their lives are not ruined forever. There is still hope and light at the end of the tunnel for individuals in a terminated marriage.

I once heard the married friends of a divorced couple ask, "Who gets us in the divorce?" As funny as this sounds, there is a bit of truth in it.

One issue couples often face is how to separate from someone and end the marriage when they have made so many connections as a direct result of the marriage. There are friendships that were created within the marriage. Property was purchased and traditions were established. To end all this is a devastating thing. If there are children involved, then it becomes exponentially more difficult.

But leaving a marriage doesn't mean you have to discard everything that was ever associated with the marriage. Starting over doesn't always have to be a brand-new start. Some of the things you acquired are a part of your life, and there should be a way to keep them intact.

Ending a marriage always causes collateral damage. Having to manage that damage can often be devastating for an individual if they don't have a clear plan on how to proceed.

The first thing to understand is that you don't have to eliminate people out of your life as though they don't exist. Besides, let's be real. If there are serious family connections, this is almost impossible for most people to do, as much as you would like to drop that person off the face of the earth.

The better alternative is to understand how to categorize

relationships. When you are choosing to end a relationship, it's essential to know how to create distance. There is a delicate balance you must achieve so you can do what is necessary to handle familial responsibilities and still keep sane, all while protecting your heart.

There are four categories of relationships: primary, proximate, peripheral, and public. When these are clearly understood, you can know how to manage the people in your life. These classifications can go a long way in helping you to reduce the drama that always follows a breakup.

Let's look at them individually.

Primary Relationships

These are the essential relationships in your life. These are the people closest to you; the ones who matter the most and without whom your life would be significantly affected. Primary relationships may be spouses, relatives, or even a best friend. They are the people you contact when you have joys and tragedies. They know your secrets and where all the bodies are buried.

This is the inner circle of your life. Usually, only a small number of people can occupy this space—your spouse, best friends, children, and so on. When a spouse has been your primary friend and then is no longer there because of divorce or separation, the result can be devastating.

Placing a person in a *primary* position means there is an understood mutual trust and dependence. The relationship is not one-sided. Both parties enjoy the comfort of personal closeness. This is not a place in your relationship world that you treat carelessly. It is a privilege to have someone as a primary relationship. They know you. They understand how you think and what you're thinking. You may even finish each other's sentences. They honestly celebrate your successes and genuinely mourn your losses.

I advise you to protect and honor this category, because not everyone is fortunate and blessed to live here.

Proximate Relationships

The proximate relationships in your life are close relationships that are valuable and desirable but are not mandatory for your personal happiness and contentment. These are the friends you have met as a result of your marriage. They may be the people you call occasionally to share a good story or some of the ones you may invite to dinner parties or events.

The proximate people are different from primary in that they don't know the most intimate parts of your life. They are close but not too close. Friendly but not too friendly.

Marriages over years will develop many proximate relationships. These are people who have made couple connections, but not necessarily close individual ones. These relationships are socially important. You may have deep conversations on occasion, and friends may even feel as though you are close. But I've found that close friends (*proximate*) will often have other closer friends who are primary.

When a proximate relationship ends, there may be brief periods of grief or sadness. You may be affected by a feeling of loss or even nostalgia, but it is usually short-lived. You will recover because that person didn't have deep roots in your intimate world. You will be hurt but not devastated.

Peripheral Relationships

These are the most common type of relationships or acquaintances. They exist on the margins or the outskirts of your life. We often find these at our places of business or in casual social settings. Peripheral relationships may exist with your neighbors whom you see regularly but don't remember their names. They are task-driven relationships.

You do not include peripheral relationships in your private business. They generally do not know or remember your children's names or even where you live. These are acquaintances or associates; they could include social media friends you may have attended school with or worked with at some time. They bring some joy when you're in contact, but you rarely initiate interaction because the relationships don't have depth. They may not call to wish you happy birthday. They will connect with you only if there is a reason, not because there is a relationship.

People in this category are not a significant or important part of your life. They are not as close as proximate relationships. When these relationships are severed or the people are no longer in your world, you may remember them, but you don't truly grieve.

Public Relationships

The public relationship is that which exists in the general population. This area is reserved for people who no longer have a right to participate in your relationship world. They are not allowed private entry into your inner circles.

It is a drastic thing to place someone in the public classification.

Often these are the people who have caused you some harm or you may have determined are completely toxic. It is clear they cannot exist in your presence, and you both understand it.

Most people find it difficult to relegate anyone to what I call the relationship black hole of existence. When you have sentenced someone to the public classification, you choose not to have contact with that person. Also, you are not affected when the relationship is severed.

Public relationships consist of people you may or not know. When you have placed someone in this group, they are at the farthest possible distance from you. While this is not pleasant, it is necessary in a lot of cases.

A NEW WAY OF LIVING

When you move forward with a divorce, you will have to adapt to a new way of living at every level described above.

The first thing to consider is that each category is a relationship. In spite of where you choose to place a person in your life, each classification still constitutes a relationship. There is still a connection, albeit tangential in the case of the public relationships. The point here is to realize that once a person enters your life in any way, there is an effect. So you have to choose where people belong based on how you are affected.

Sarah had to make sure she kept some contact with her ex-husband, Levi, because they had children together. However, their circumstances were such that she had difficulty being around him and his new baby. Subsequently, she decided he was not allowed to bring the baby or the new mother to her home.

While the baby was innocent, Sarah had to draw boundaries she could live with. She had to take control to determine where people would fit in her life. It was the right thing to do for her and the kids until time could allow some healing to occur.

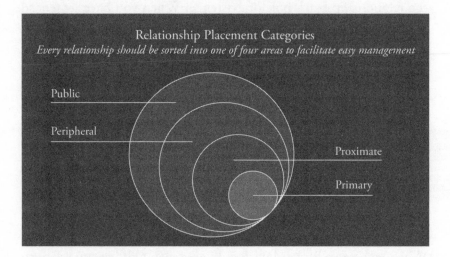

These decisive actions are imperative when it comes to severing a relationship as powerful as marriage. There has to be an intentional decision as to where people fit. While it may not seem equitable or fair in the eyes of some, everyone has to figure out what's comfortable for them, because when there is no decision, and everything is just allowed to happen, it causes a great deal of confusion and frustration.

One thing I have always encouraged couples to do is get counseling, especially when they are about to divorce. They need pre-divorce counseling so that they can leave a relationship on civil terms and understand where this former life partner now fits in their new life. Often, I've sat in front of couples who have decided that they could not get beyond infidelity. Their marital experience was just too toxic and injurious to them and the only solution was to leave.

It is at this time that intervention is needed more than ever. It's not easy to revert back to a single mindset when you have embraced being a couple for so long. But this is the time when you actually must know how to categorize the people in your life. And the most important but most difficult thing to do is take control of how and when your former spouse should be in your life.

Again, I usually try to use every trick in the book to get couples to work it out, but when they reach an inevitable and sometimes necessary impasse, I show them how to take control of their new way of living. They must realize they have control of where people are placed in their lives. They are the arbiters of how close their ex should be and how much, if any, emotional investment will be allowed.

You can never allow another person to determine when and how they should be in your life. No one gets to write the agenda for your new life but you. So it's fundamental that you take control and communicate where your ex is being placed. Don't leave any room for speculation.

The other point to consider is that the categories must remain clearly defined and separated. It must be clearly communicated that this is the new arrangement. The ex must be informed as to what they are allowed to do and what they are prohibited from doing.

Being too nice in such a moment can be disastrous. If Sarah had relaxed her guard and just allowed Levi to create the agenda and determine the boundaries, it would have caused too much drama for all involved. Their children needed a peaceful place while adjusting to this new way of life. Their home could not become a battleground. Levi was not a primary figure in Sarah's life anymore, so he didn't have the privileges he used to enjoy. He could not hold a public position and act like a primary relationship.

This is one of the more difficult points to understand when categorizing relationships. If someone is in a public or peripheral class, you should not invite them to intimate events. A person whom you may see only occasionally would be surprised or bewildered to receive an invitation to your intimate dinner party. In fact, they may feel it's a mistake and not respond.

Conversely, your primary friends don't need permission to call you or come over. They don't maintain the distance of public or peripheral people, and they are closer than proximate relationships. These are the people who clearly know they are your closest companions.

> Relationships are best enjoyed when they are best understood.

The separation of these categories is what keeps order in your life. Relationships are best enjoyed when they are best understood. It is essential to know who the people are who are closest to you and to know the ones who are not. When this is done, there is no guessing about relationships.

Now, these classifications are not written in cement. Over the course of time, positions can shift. In a number of instances, a person who was close to you in your youth may now only be a distant acquaintance. Or vice versa.

Sarah needed Levi to be public for a while until she could find healing for her hurt. After some time and once the children start to normalize the new situation, she may feel it necessary to promote him to a proximate position. This happens quite often with divorced couples. I've known many couples who had an intense hatred during the divorce, but over time it dissipated, and they were able to become cordial. Then, after new relationships were established, cordiality became friendship. So in essence, the ex was promoted from public to peripheral to proximate. However, it takes time and a serious restructuring of the relationship for this to happen.

No rational person enters a marriage expecting it to end. For the myriad of couples we've coached over the years, they all anticipated the absolute best. But sometimes our best-laid plans can be upended when conflict is allowed to build without any resolution.

When a couple gets to the point when they feel there is a greater overall benefit to everyone involved to leave, knowing how to do it skillfully can significantly reduce the fallout and collateral damage that often happens to people closely related to the marriage. Understanding the right time to leave and the right way to do so can hasten the healing from a broken relationship.

Then, once you have severed the marriage, placing your spouse in the proper category can contribute to a positive and civil postnuptial relationship. The goal is to exit the marriage and yet preserve the relationship at some level. After all, the commitment to success, the passion to enjoy one another, and the value that you held for each other meant a lot at one time.

Even through the pain of separation, you should have learned valuable skills to make yourself more equipped for your future. The benefits and emotional fulfillment experienced in the relationship should be a reminder that, at one point in time, you were united with this person, and during that union, there were positive experiences that changed you both for the better.

Acknowledgments

This book is based on over a decade of experiences, tough life lessons, counseling sessions, and spiritual revelations. I want to start by thanking my beautiful wife Wendy, who has consistently been my encourager, my best friend, my muse, and my ride or die chick. Your heart and mind are intricately woven throughout these pages. I could have never done this and would have never had the desire to do this without you. I love you beyond words. I would also like to thank our children who have taught us patience, even though it was not their intention to do so. But their growth, their intelligence, their trust in me as a father and even their challenges have taught me volumes about responsibility and life.

Thank you to my mother, who at the writing of this acknowledgement is about to celebrate her one-hundred-year birthday. You have given me strength and taught me how to be faithful beyond all else. God bless you.

Thanks to my friends, who have challenged me and kept me normalized by knowing my deepest secrets. If in life you have one great friend, you are blessed. I have been blessed exponentially by having all of you in my life.

I would also like to thank the myriad of couples I've coached and counseled over the past decades. Just being a listener to your challenges and helping guide you through your personal journeys has been an immeasurable contributor to the knowledge I've been able to relay to others in this book. Though your privacy has been carefully protected, I want you to know that your successes and struggles will now help others to become whole.

I'm so grateful and thankful to the best church family in the world, Progression Church. You guys have been my spiritual support and have been a source of joy, inspiration, and motivation. May you continue to thrive. This is for us!

Also, an incredible thanks to the *Marriage Ain't for Punks* team. You guys believed in me and took this project on with enthusiasm and vigor. My agents, Byrd Leavell and Josh Levenbrown, you guys have been no less than awesome. The team at Hachette Books (FaithWords) has been efficient, professional, and encouraging. Thank you all so much. This literally would not have happened without you.

Most important I would like to thank God. Even as I write these words, I sense that You understand the depth of those simple words of eternal gratitude.

About the Author

Calvin Roberson is a television relationship expert, public speaker, church pastor, author, and award-winning entrepreneur. He received his bachelor of arts from Oakwood University and master's of divinity from Andrews University. A Virginia native, he is the husband to his beauty queen, and the father of three brilliant children. He has been privileged to serve as an NYSE financial representative, a regional vice president of an international financial services company, an international public speaker, the dean of a world-renowned arts school, a successful marriage coach, and a television star. His passion lies in transcribing his thoughts, passions, and experiences to the written word. You can visit him online at www.calvinroberson.com.